TALES
for
COACHING

TALES *for* COACHING

**Using Stories and Metaphors with
Individuals & Small Groups**

Margaret Parkin

KOGAN
PAGE

First published in 2001

Kogan Page Limited
120 Pentonville Road
London
N1 9JN
UK

Stylus Publishing Inc.
22883 Quicksilver Drive
Sterling
VA 20166-2012
USA

British Library Cataloguing in Publication Data

A CIP record for this book is available from the British Library.

ISBN 0 7494 3521 6

Typeset by Jean Cussons Typesetting, Diss, Norfolk
Printed and bound in Great Britain by Clays Ltd, St Ives plc

Contents

Contents

Introduction

Are you a storyteller? The chances are you'll reply 'Who me? Certainly not', having in your mind a picture of some strange mediaeval creature prancing around in cap, motley and bells, or possibly of a favourite comedian or raconteur, spitting out well-rehearsed and scripted lines at the speed of light. You might even think of the word 'storyteller' in a derogatory way, as someone who is prone to exaggeration or being economical with the truth. Even dictionaries list 'storyteller' as synonymous with 'liar'.

The fact is, if you are involved in coaching, instructing, mentoring or educating other people, with a view to helping them achieve optimum performance, and if your aim is to do this in a way that is stimulating and memorable, then the chances are that you *are* incorporating some of the skills that the original storytellers crafted centuries ago: educating and entertaining their listeners, painting verbal pictures to enhance memory, using metaphor and analogy to add colour, and passing on cumulative wisdom.

If you can relate to some or all of these amazing skills then you're in good company – Aesop, Jesus Christ, William Shakespeare and Hans Christian Andersen amongst others – and the purpose of this book is to help you to develop these skills even further, to bring them up to date within a modern business context, and to show how storytelling can be used in a powerful way to enhance one-to-one or small-group coaching.

Some of you may have read my first book, *Tales for Trainers*. Its focus is how to use stories and metaphors to facilitate learning in a group training context. Shortly after it was published, a woman came up to me at a conference, clutching a copy to her chest, and said, 'I bought your book for our training department,' and then added with a shy grin, 'but I'm keeping it for myself. I use some of the stories for my own personal development.'

A few weeks later, one of my clients, another story devotee from a large retail organization, said to me, 'We bought your book for our library, so

1

that our trainers could use it for their training sessions. But we need some more copies because they borrow it and don't bring it back! I think,' she continued, conspiratorially, 'that they're reading the stories for their own personal use.'

I was surprised how many times this sort of thing happened, and it reinforced my thinking that, as well as being a powerful tool for group learning, stories also have an important part to play in individual learning, personal development and in the one-to-one coaching that can help people to achieve their goals.

The first part of this book sets the scene by putting storytelling into its historical context. It outlines the storytelling traditions and explains the purpose and benefits of stories and metaphors, with particular emphasis on personal learning.

If you are a coach, there is guidance on how to use stories, particularly in a one-to-one or small-group setting, to address such issues as goal setting, problem solving and action planning, how to build rapport with your coachee, and how to develop your storytelling voice – without sounding like you're addressing a group of four year olds!

Part two is a collection of 50 stories, metaphors, poems and anecdotes that can be used before, during or after the coaching session. As with my first book, other authors have kindly lent me some of the stories and some are written from my own experience. Others, in true storytelling fashion, are old or traditional tales that I have retold or given a 21st-century 'makeover'. Most of them take only about five minutes to read, but there are one or two in this collection that take a little longer. In coaching, when compared with large group training, I feel that there is more scope for private study and reflection prior to discussion.

Accompanying each of the stories is a 'moral' containing the learning message of the tale, and a 'reflection', that includes some useful trigger points and questions to stimulate thought. I leave it up to you as to whether you feel it appropriate to 'declare' the moral or learning message of the tale. Some storytelling purists would be horrified to think you would even consider divulging a moral. Personally I think the choice is yours. You know your coachee, the context and your desired outcome far better than I do! Some people's response to a particular story can be like a light turning on – a real 'ah ha' moment, when they can draw clear parallels between the message of the story and what is going on in their own lives. Others may still be looking perplexed half-an-hour later and you might need to prompt them to find the links – and that is where the 'reflection' questions come in. You can use these to encourage discussion, promote creative thought and allow reflection time.

The stories are grouped into the five main areas that coaches most commonly work on with their coachees, namely:

- **Envisioning and goal setting.** *'So, what do you want to achieve?'* These stories encourage people to see their mission and goals clearly, to reflect on whether a goal is indeed theirs or somebody else's, to be specific in their goal setting – and most importantly, to consider what they will do if they achieve it.
- **Problem solving.** *'How are you going to achieve it?'* Stories included in this section are to help people to appreciate their own strengths and capabilities, to give them hope to keep trying, to break down and analyse different parts of the problem and not to be afraid to apply different solutions.
- **Reframing and creativity.** *'Let's look at this another way...'* Metaphors are a great way of 'seeing things from a different perspective' and this group of stories is intended to help people to change their mindset.
- **Empowerment.** *'You can do it!'* Very often people do not achieve all they want because they become disempowered, in other words, it's easier to wait for someone else to do it – and then complain about it! This section contains stories to encourage people to realize that they always have some degree of choice in what they do.
- **Success and self-esteem.** *'I told you that you could do it!'* One of the most common things that holds people back in their own development is a feeling of low self-esteem, and this inspiring set of stories will encourage people to believe in themselves – their greatest resource!

One of the hardest things to do when compiling an anthology of just 50 tales is to limit yourself in choosing the stories to include and those to miss out. The world (thankfully) is full of stories, and in the last few years, so many of them, in all their various shapes, sizes and colours, have come parading like some joyful Caribbean carnival to my door, pleading to be let in. But rest assured that at least one of the things that all these stories has in common is that they only pass the entrance exam if they have been tried and tested by myself and others in coaching situations, and are found to be effective, thought provoking and offering a stimulating way of learning. So... let's open the door and let the carnival begin...

PART ONE

Are You Sitting Comfortably?

CHAPTER 1

Introducing Storytelling

THE STORY BEGINS

Are you sitting comfortably? I hope so, because if you are it means that you recognize that well-known phrase, probably from your childhood days, as heralding the beginning of a story. Indeed, that's just what this book is about: it's a story about storytelling, from its ancient beginnings and original purpose to, most importantly, the part it has to play today in the modern business world – particularly for those of us whose role involves coaching, training and the development of others.

If you are sitting comfortably, in eager anticipation, you can consider yourself to be part of an age-old tradition that dates back to the beginning of time – well before the birth of Christ and certainly prior to the advent of the written word. Indeed, this was the original and primary function of storytelling. It was the means of passing on information and knowledge orally from one person to another, or from one tribe to another, or from one village to another, in much the same way as we currently rely on television, radio, newspapers or the Internet to keep us up to date and help us make sense of what is going on in the world.

Storytelling has always been an essential and universal human characteristic. The history of every society in every part of the world includes its own version of storytelling – and most societies continue to have storytelling activities in some shape or form today. Over the years, storytellers themselves have taken on many different names and guises throughout the world – *griots* in West Africa, *troubadours* and *minstrels* in Western Europe, *pandits* in Hindu India, *bards* in the Celtic world.

During the Middle Ages, people began to realize just how dependent they were on the storytellers for reliable information and knowledge, and as their power and influence became apparent, the profession itself gained in respect and admiration. Some storytellers were frequent visitors at court, and were recognized as highly influential with the king or queen of the time. Very often it was the jester who was the only member of court who could get away with telling the truth – albeit cleverly veiled in the guise of a joke or story – without having his head cut off! Using bizarre animals as story characters helped these early storytellers to satirize the political events of the day; they could make fun of their leaders without fear of retribution. And so, fables and allegories and metaphors were born, and thousands of years later, we are still using them. Although they now might be in a different format – situation comedy, political satire or pantomime – their intention is still to point out the follies and frailties of human behaviour.

Good storytellers found themselves to be much in demand during the Middle Ages, which naturally led to many of them becoming quite affluent. In some cultures it was even seen as something of a status symbol – whether you could afford a professional storyteller for your tribal gathering – in just the same way that for some children in our modern day culture a party isn't a proper party without the hiring of Mr Chuckles, the child entertainer, and just as some organizations would feel cheated without the obligatory motivational rousing of the 'after dinner speaker'.

However, as with all high-profile jobs, along with the fame and fortune came the acceptance of responsibility, and in some cultures, the storytellers, prior to being allowed to practise their art, were actually required to take a solemn vow, in which they declared that any information they passed on to others would be:

- accurate;
- interesting;
- memorable.

Indeed, in some modern-day storytelling societies the same sort of vows still apply, and any would-be storyteller has to commit to abiding by them. Just think what a difference it might make to the quality of the communication within organizations if this was a pledge that could be introduced there!

The simple passing on of topical information was not the only function performed by the original storytellers. They also had an important role to play in building communities, and preserving and sharing historical data. In ancient times, tribes would gather round their campfires at night to tell stories of their heroic deeds and accomplishments. These stories would then be passed on from one to another and would gradually spread, like a ripple effect, to more and more people within the community. Eventually everyone would be talking a shared language that came to represent the tribe's cultural values and history, which in turn helped them to make sense of their world and their part in it.

Today, although people in organizations might gather round the photo-copier or in the staff restaurant rather than round an actual 'campfire', the process of swapping stories with each other is just the same as it was a thousand years ago – and it serves the same important function. People laughing or crying together at the sharing of a story builds the community and bonds people together.

The original storytellers were also involved in education and the transfer of cumulative wisdom, which ensured the continuity of experience from one generation to the next. In communities the world over there has been, and still is, a tradition of the old educating the young. Milbre Burch, a storyteller in Pasadena, California, says:

> Storytelling has its roots in the tribal traditions of oral cultures back when memory was the library. Elders passed on their wisdom through the vessel of story. Storytelling is still transgenerational today – it appeals to multi-age audiences.
>
> (Burch, 1997)

In our modern-day organizations we can still witness this transfer of cumulative wisdom, when those people whom anthropologist Peg Neuhauser (1993) refers to as 'the tribal elders' (highly respected or senior members of the organization) are called upon to share their memories as part of an induction or orientation programme to educate new employees in 'the way we do things'. If these stories are told positively and enthusiastically, in line with good storytelling traditions, and, most importantly, are congruent with organizational behaviour, their effects can be far more powerful and believable than any corporate video, newsletter or handbook that you might employ. Researchers have shown personal storytelling to be the most credible and memorable form of communication.

However, if the stories are incompatible with organizational behaviour, then both storyteller and story lose all credibility. Peg Neuhauser goes on to say: 'If you tell a story to illustrate facts, events or "the way things are done around here", and the story does not match the listeners' experience, the stories are likely to be rejected.'

I worked once with a human resources director who, on the same day that he very piously told a group of trainee managers how important it was, in performance management, *never to act rashly* when making a decision that affected others, dismissed an employee on the spot for 'his negative attitude' and was later taken to court for unfair dismissal. His particular brand of storytelling and related behaviour became legendary – for the wrong reasons!

In ancient Eastern cultures, storytelling was used particularly as a gentle yet powerful form of counselling and therapy. In those days, if a person visited the doctor suffering from depression, rather than receiving a prescription for Prozac or another anti-depressant that we might expect today, it was common practice for the doctor to 'prescribe' a fairy story, myth or traditional tale, which bore some similarity to the patient's own dilemma and on which they were expected to meditate. It was felt that contemplation of the story would provide the patient with a metaphor or different perspective to consider and offer clarity to the problem that he or she was facing. In his book, *The Uses of Enchantment*, Bruno Bettelheim (1991) says:

> The figures and events of fairy tales also personify and illustrate inner conflicts, but they suggest ever so subtly how these conflicts may be solved, and what the next steps in the development toward a higher humanity might be.
>
> (Bettelheim, 1991)

Traditional stories can often provide a source of comfort for the listener by introducing a 'helper', 'guide' or other protective person, who always appears just at the right moment, in order to help the protagonist on his/her journey. The helper can take many forms – a fairy godmother, a guardian angel, a Buddha – or perhaps some sort of conscience figure who stands on your shoulder and whispers advice in your ear.

In the field of therapy, this tradition has been carried on very successfully into contemporary practice. Therapists have for some time accepted and used storytelling as an effective yet non-invasive form of therapy. In the 1960s and 1970s, Milton Erickson was renowned for his use of metaphorical 'teaching tales' that would amuse, surprise or even shock clients into affecting some change in their lives. The neurolinguistic programming (NLP) school and Gestalt school of therapy all include stories and metaphors as part of their toolkit for creative thinking and problem solving.

These then were – and still remain – the three main functions of storytelling:

- to pass on information and knowledge;
- to educate and encourage the transfer of cumulative wisdom from one generation to the next;
- to encourage personal healing and creative problem solving.

Until the mid 1400s, storytelling was riding high in popularity and doing very nicely, thank you. After Gutenberg invented his printing press in 1450, people became far more interested in seeing stories in print and the storytelling profession understandably took something of a drop in terms of its popularity and perceived usefulness. In a famous essay entitled, 'The Storyteller' written in 1936, Walter Benjamin took a pessimistic view of the future of storytelling:

> The art of storytelling is coming to an end. Less and less frequently do we encounter people with an ability to tell a tale properly. More and more often there is embarrassment all around when a wish to tell a story is expressed.
>
> (Benjamin, quoted in Rosen, 1987)

One might easily believe that to be true, particularly with the advent of radio, television and film – and now, of course, information technology and all that that brings. One could say that in modern times, the apparent need for an oral storyteller has almost evaporated, except that, paradoxically, over the last fifty years storytelling activity is actually on the increase! Jack Zipes, Professor at the University of Minnesota and Patron of the Society for Storytelling, says:

> Storytelling is everywhere – in the schools and libraries, in homes and in the TV tubes, in the pubs and restaurants, during the lunch breaks, in airports and train stations, on the phone, in the theatres and cinemas. Contrary to what Benjamin believed, storytelling was not about to perish in the 1930s and certainly does not appear to be on the verge of perishing today.
>
> (Zipes, 1996)

In fact, since the 1970s in particular there has been a steady increase in the number of professional and semi-professional storytellers throughout the world, and an equal number of societies and organizations to help them do it. (See the back of this book for a list of the best known.) There are also a growing number of storytelling festivals, symposia and workshops operating around the world. The public-speaking organization, Toastmasters International, recently added 'storytelling' as an advanced programme in its portfolio.

So, why is it that, despite all our present-day sophisticated methods of communication (or is it because of it?), people are still telling stories, whether it be one-to-one or in small groups or large audiences, as they have done for thousands of years? There is no one definitive answer, except to say that:

- There is obviously still faith in storytelling as a means of communication otherwise it simply would not have survived; people would have stopped using it.
- Storytelling as a means of taking in and making sense of information is an interactive and sharing process, and is therefore more powerful than a passive means, such as the images one soaks up from a television or computer.

- People are now realizing the full potential and possible applications of this ancient and influential art in the modern world.

HOW DO STORIES WORK?

Stories and metaphors can enhance learning and memory

The challenge for the original storytellers was that, before writing was invented, there was no other way of backing up the verbal information that they gave to other people. Just put yourself in that position: with no letters, memorandums, e-mail or books at your disposal, how would you ensure that the information you gave to people was *accurate, interesting* and most importantly *memorable* to comply with the storyteller's original vow? If you were attempting to pass on your wisdom so that others could learn and benefit from it, how would you ensure that the lesson had actually been taken in and understood?

First of all, in order to remember the information themselves, the storytellers had to be able to use their brains in a way that was distinctly different to that of their contemporaries. Over time, they developed heightened listening and speaking skills, an understanding and insight into current affairs and probably most importantly, an advanced capacity for memory and visualization – similar skills to those of a modern-day coach you might say. Storytellers discovered, originally through trial and error, that the best way to remember and make sense of information was to create vivid and fantastic images in their minds and weave the information into them.

They also found that the memory techniques they used on themselves, which we would now call memory-enhancing visualization, worked just as well in getting the message across to their listeners. In fact, in some cultures, storytellers of different tribes competed with one another to come up with the most creative, bizarre and captivating tales – hence the birth of wicked witches, flying dragons and talking pigs – ensuring that there were no limits to the imagination! What the original storytellers were doing instinctively has since been confirmed by contemporary brain research. Learning and memory work best when:

- the information is seen as part of a *context or bigger picture*;
- *novelty and interest* are generated;
- *emotions* are involved.

Learning through context or the bigger picture

Our brains are just like heat-seeking missiles: they automatically search out meaning, context and patterns in the world. The neocortex is the part of the brain that deals with our intellectual processes such as thinking and talking. Its primary function is to take all the apparently meaningless bits of data that enter our heads and fit them into some sort of pattern or 'perceptual map' that helps us to understand. The neocortex is both a pattern maker and pattern detector; it can sort and store information using a system far more complex than the most powerful computer. It plays a crucial role in the learning process. When we learn something new, the neocortex either makes an association with an existing pattern (assimilating) or creates a new one (structurizing), which it then puts into storage in our unconscious minds for retrieval at a later date.

Boller and Rovee-Collier (1992) found that when students learnt about a subject as part of a context – through a story, map or perspective relevant to the topic – learning and memory dramatically improved. Offering a context or conceptual framework for learning allows learners to make connections with what they consider to be important to them and boosts their memory recall. This is also why children prefer being told stories with lots of repetition, sometimes known as 'cumulative tales' – for example 'The Twelve Days of Christmas' and 'The House That Jack Built'. It helps them to establish and confirm the patterns in their brains – and they will soon tell you if you get the words wrong!

In a coaching situation, just telling coachees something, or dropping them a line with the instruction *'be a good manager'*, although quick and cheap would be a sterile, dull and meaningless way of learning, and certainly wouldn't guarantee positive results. To learn specific aspects of the role of management through the medium of a story offers a bigger context and can be so much richer, thought provoking and memorable. It is a well-known saying that 'experience makes a good teacher' and if stories are based on experience – your own or other people's – then they must be the next best thing to learning through real life.

> Natural language stories (when understood by us 'empathically') demonstrably affect our brain systems. Such language reminds us and evokes much the same response in our brain systems as would experiencing what the speaker tells about. In this respect mathematical–logical language does not work evocatively.
>
> (Bartter, Hilgartner, and Stoneman, 1999)

Stories themselves can contain patterns and templates that help us to put things into context. These patterns might be contained in the stories of our own lives, or in the stories and metaphors of others. Kaye and

Jacobson (1999) say that if we see 'the multiple incidents of our lives as essential parts of a pattern, we find value in the stories that created the pattern'. In other words, we are more likely to discover some meaning in our own lives if we view events as being part of a bigger picture rather than a series of random mishaps. This helps us to apply the learning to future events.

When listening to other people's stories, it may be that the pattern of a problem or issue that your coachee is currently dealing with can be seen to be paralleled with the pattern or template contained in the story. For example, you might tell your coachee a story of someone else who had a similar problem and how he or she dealt with it. Or you might choose a traditional tale or anecdote containing a relevant metaphor. When the coachees recognize the pattern (albeit unconsciously) and make the connection, their self-knowledge is enhanced and they discover new ways of dealing with the problem.

Learning through novelty and interest

It may almost seem like a contradiction to the last heading, but learning and memory can also be enhanced when information is presented in a novel, out-of-the-ordinary way that doesn't fit with the established patterns and templates in our brains. McGaugh *et al* (1990) said that when any information does not fit into an existing and recognizable pattern it is immediately catalogued by the neocortex as *different*, the natural stress levels are raised and all sorts of alarm bells start ringing! If the information is perceived as a negative threat, the body may release cortisol; if it's perceived as positive then adrenaline is released. McGaugh *et al* found from their experiments that both of these chemicals actually work like memory fixatives and that people could remember far longer than when the chemicals were not present.

This is the way in which metaphors can work so powerfully in our minds. A metaphor can be anything from a word or short phrase – 'it's a nightmare', 'she's living life in the fast lane', 'he's a teddy bear' – to a complete story, which is often described as an 'extended metaphor'. A metaphor is a comparison between two sometimes completely unrelated subjects, and it is this very difference that can create a tension or dissonance in our minds that requires resolution – or as creative thinker Roger von Oeuch (1998) might say (metaphorically) it gives us 'a whack on the side of the head'!

Listening to a metaphor serves as a 'pattern interrupt', which means that it gives us a '*What??*' sort of experience, and jolts us out of our logical, habitual thinking. It can also bypass our natural resistance to change. If coachees perceive that they are being told what to do or given advice, then there is always a danger that the protective barriers will come up. Being offered possible solutions through the medium of a metaphor is more acceptable and non-threatening and there is less perceived pressure to accept the advice being offered.

For a metaphor to work best there has to be just enough distance between the two subjects (known as the 'topic' and the 'vehicle') for the listener to be able to make some connection, but not so close as to appear over obvious or too far away as to appear obtuse. For example, *'she's living life in the fast lane'* works because we all have some understanding of the concept of a fast lane – whether it be on a motorway or an athletic track – and what that might mean in relation to a person's life. But to say *'she's living life as a football'* probably would not work because it is too distant and there is too little in the way of comparison for us to relate to.

The vivid and colourful imagery of metaphor is what helps us to remember the information and expand our learning potential. Its appropriate use can bring about a deeper, insightful understanding of ourselves and others. 'A large part of self-understanding is the search for appropriate personal metaphors that make sense of our lives' (Lakoff and Johnson, 1980).

We should always be careful, when introducing a metaphor to our coachees, to choose one that is appropriate, relevant and sensitive to them rather than picking an image that just serves for our own benefit and amusement (see Chapter 3 for advice on choosing stories and metaphors). Don't make the mistake that a colleague of mine did some years ago when she (quite unwittingly) talked to a coachee about a 'meaty' illustration to a problem, only to discover that he was a staunch vegetarian who was most offended by the reference!

Stories, anecdotes or analogies can all be seen as extended metaphors, and you will find this to be one of the common denominators of the stories in Part Two of this book. The general format and structure of any story, whether it be a short anecdote or a full-length fairytale or myth, is basically the same. The character(s) in the story (real or imaginary) encounter some sort of problem, conflict or challenge (the dissonance), which they deal with, either successfully or unsuccessfully, thereby achieving a resolution of some sort. Nigel Watts (1996) describes this format as a series of points or milestones on a journey:

1. The status quo – where we join the hero/heroine.
2. The trigger – something happens that means the status quo cannot continue.
3. The quest – the response to the challenge.
4. The surprise – what really slaps us in the face.
5. The critical choice – the dilemma.

6. The climax – the choice we make.
7. The reversal – the change that results from the choice we make.
8. The resolution – if the reversal is sustained.

These stages of a story can provide a useful parallel for coachees in terms of any 'journey' that they might be making, particularly one that involves a challenge or problem, for example, a change of job, promotion, setting new goals or horizons, or a change in domestic circumstances. If the conflict in the story is seen to be similar to the one that the coachee is dealing with, then the message of the story takes on more significance. The notion of using stories in this way as a tool for self-transformation has been a widely held view in the therapeutic world for some time. This topic is explored more in Chapter 2.

Learning with emotions

Researchers such as Ornstein, Sperry and Lakoff have proved, through repeated studies into the workings of the brain, that learning and memory are enhanced by being associated with emotional activity. Because the emotional centre of the brain (the limbic system) is situated closely to the part responsible for long-term memory storage, we all remember more easily when our emotions have been aroused, whether it be excitement, curiosity, anger or suspense. In addition, O'Keefe and Nadel (1978) found that experiencing positive emotions makes it easier for us to make better 'perceptual maps'. That is, we can recall and make sense of our thoughts and experiences more clearly and accurately.

More recently, researchers like Daniel Goleman (1999), author of *Working with Emotional Intelligence,* and Jack Canfield (1996), author of *Heart at Work* and *Chicken Soup for the Soul* series, brought into our awareness the fact that, in a business context, simply using our intellectual and technical ability is no longer enough to succeed in today's organizations. The qualities that we should now be focusing on and developing are the 'personal' skills, such as initiative and empathy, self-esteem and motivation. In other words, we need to be aware of and manage our emotions – and stories can help us to do that in a way that other means of communication can't. A well-told story can trigger positive feelings of curiosity, surprise or excitement, or negative feelings of sadness, depression or anger, far more than say a column of figures or other sequential lists and reports. Stories can shock, too. Therapist Milton Erickson was well-known for his use of teaching tales, some specifically designed to shock his clients out of a habitual pattern of behaviour (see 'Style' on p 139).

Stories by themselves are neither positive nor negative – it depends on how they are used and for what purpose. Peg Neuhauser (1993), in her book *Corporate Legends and Lore*, says that we need to focus on the *intended outcome* of a story to determine whether it produces a positive or negative emotion. To do this, we can analyse or evaluate the effectiveness of hearing a story by asking questions such as:

- Did people feel proud of themselves or others on hearing the story?
- Did the story help the teller and listener(s) to let off steam or reduce stress?
- Did the story shock or shake people up?

If I ask a coachee to give me an example of customer service that they have received, and give them the choice of telling a positive or negative story, the story they invariably choose is one of poor service, and this is perceived by them to be a negative story. However, when you investigate their reasons for telling it, it is very often that they personally emerge from the drama as being the 'conquering hero' who rises to the challenge of 'sorting it out' – whether 'it' is the postman, the next-door neighbour, the organization or the telephone bill – and triumphs, in spite of great adversity, like David over Goliath. So the story is actually evoking positive emotions both for the individual telling it – and, if this is done in a group, for those listening because they can relate to the experiences that they hear and are quick to volunteer ones of their own. Group storytelling like this can go on for hours! But due to the fact that the emotions have been aroused you will find that these incidents will be remembered – which is why it is important for you as a coach to ensure that the positive learning aspect of any story is stressed. The use of positive emotion in a story, when done well, can be very contagious and uplifting. Michael Hattersley (1997) in his article on the managerial art of telling a story, says:

> Stories can be the best way to package meaning and spur others on to achieve. At the most basic level, storytelling can help a manager gain and hold his audience's attention. But if the story is good enough, it can also lift individuals and organizations to take the risks that keep life an adventure.
> (Hattersley, 1997)

Learning with humour

Humour is an emotion that deserves a special mention. Although very difficult to analyse (and God forbid that we should!) humour has been proved to be a powerful partner in the learning business. Indeed, many video companies in the 1970s and 1980s were built on the basis of using humorous stories to teach dry or academic subjects.

Eric Jensen (1988) documents some work carried out at Indiana University, where researchers found that when learners were exposed to humour they were more receptive to information and there was better rapport between the teacher and the learner. They also found that when students were given key learning points, *followed* by a humorous story, they remembered the key points much better than when there was no story. Which coincidentally reminds me of a funny story...

When I was working with children in school years ago, I was listening to a group reciting its 'two times table':

One two is two,
Two twos are four,
Three twos are six,
Four twos are eight...

As they carried on in that monotonous and rhythmical chant peculiar to children, I noticed a little boy at the back of the room, who was clearly somewhat out of synch with the rest of the class. His version was more along the lines of:

Du du du daaah,
Du du du daaah...

When I asked him the reason for this variation, he replied cheerily, 'Oh I know the tune, Miss, I just can't remember the words!' Clearly, learning by 'rote' doesn't always guarantee understanding!

Whenever we laugh, our brains are stimulated to produce cate-cholamine, an alertness hormone, which in turn brings about the release of endorphins, the body's own natural pain killers. So, as well as having great potential for our general well-being and physical healing, laughter can have the same effect on our brains as taking a tranquillizer – although happily it's usually cheaper and has less harmful side effects!

Humour can be used very effectively in both one-to-one and small group coaching, although you have to make sure that the content and flavour is *appropriate*, in other words, the humour should be shared and enjoyed by everyone equally. In my view, you should only introduce humour when you have good rapport with your listener(s) and it should certainly never be used to intentionally wound, ridicule or alienate. People enjoying a funny story and laughing together is a great way to defuse any tension that might exist, and in a group coaching session it can also help to build a sense of community within the members.

STORIES AND UNCONSCIOUS LEARNING

German poet and philosopher Goethe said: 'The maturity of a human being is to return to the seriousness of the child at play.' If you've ever watched children playing, you'll know that it is a serious business that requires their full concentration. As adults, listening to and becoming totally engrossed in a story, which happens quite easily if the story is told well, can help to reduce stress and muscle tension and promote feelings of well-being and relaxation. Carter Liggett at the Pacific Graduate School of Psychology in California carried out tests on the saliva of story-listeners, and discovered that these people actually experienced a biochemical change whilst listening – their levels of cortisol (the stress hormone) dropped and levels of immunoglobulin A rose.

When people are relaxed, they are naturally more receptive, which in turn helps them to learn and retain information more easily. Brain scans and research into the different functions and activities of the brain have shown that our brains work on four different wavelengths or frequencies:

- Beta – the conscious, wide-awake brain.
- Alpha – the state of relaxed awareness.
- Theta – on the edge of sleep.
- Delta – deep sleep.

Although we might think that our conscious, wide-awake brains would be the best state for learning, research has shown that, in fact, we absorb information much more quickly and effectively when our brains are at alpha level, or in a state of 'relaxed awareness'. Listening to a story is of course an enjoyable and effective way of achieving this state. American storyteller Milbre Burch says: 'Storytelling is more than a spectator sport. Often engaged in a light trance state, the listener co-creates the story with the teller' (Burch, 1997).

The power of the story lies in the fact that, while our conscious minds are absorbed, the unconscious mind is free to take in the moral or message that the story contains.

This absorption in a story can also produce the effect that Chicago psychologist Mihaly Csikszentmihalyi (1990) calls 'flow'. This is the feeling you might have when you're so engrossed in an activity that you lose all notion of time, space and self, and just become one with the activity. Anyone who is learning how to use the Internet, and suddenly looks up to find they have been 'surfing' for three hours will understand the concept of 'flow'! This state, Csikszentmihalyi says, is the *optimum state for learning*. It is best achieved when the following conditions are met:

- High challenges – not too easy, not too hard, intrinsically motivated, your own choice.
- Low stress – not *no* stress, just minimal stress, a general feeling of relaxation.
- Immersed 'flow' state – attention is focused on learning and doing, not focused on self or evaluation of task.

Original research carried out by Roger Sperry in the 1960s into the functions of the two brain hemispheres also provides us with insight into the value of storytelling in unconscious learning. Simplistically, we think of the left hemisphere as being responsible for language, logic and sequence, and the right hemisphere for music, pictures and daydreaming – although in reality it is far more complicated than that and it would be wrong to try to draw up demarcation lines between the two. More recent research shows that, although it is believed that the left brain processes information faster than the right, in fact both sides of the brain are involved to some degree in most human activities, and as coaches we should encourage the development of both.

Arthur Deikman (1982) in his book *The Observing Self* suggests that the content of a story can appeal to both left and right hemispheres of the brain equally, the left processing the words sequentially and analytically, and the right dealing with visualization and pattern recognition. This means that the left side reduces its usual level of dominance over the right, allowing a greater degree of creativity and freedom.

The more that we, as coaches, can use this knowledge, the more our coachees will be able to access both hemispheres, and consequently the more proficiently they will be able to function.

CHAPTER 2

Coaching and Storytelling

COACHING – THE STORY SO FAR

For thousands of years people have been passing on their knowledge and skills to others. Since the first caveman sat down with another caveman and, holding a flint spearhead in his hand, said, 'Look, you do it this way' or more probably 'Uuggh!' (that's a colloquial translation obviously), coaching has been accepted and valued as a tried and tested means of passing on knowledge, skills and wisdom to other people.

Thirty years ago, in what were very often autocratic and hierarchical organizations, an apprentice would have typically learnt his or her craft by what was then referred to in the United Kingdom as 'sitting by Nellie'. This meant that you spent time shadowing an experienced person in the job, and basically picked up the required skills from them – in other words they coached you. And although it was an accepted practice in most industries, it never really achieved high profile and was certainly never what an advertising or marketing person might have called 'sexy' as a learning methodology.

In the last 10 years or so, trends in employment and work-based learning have changed dramatically, and coaching itself has taken on a new identity. It has become more prevalent, more structured, one might even say more fashionable as a means of enhancing learning and effecting change. Eric Parsloe, Director of the Oxford School of Coaching and Mentoring in the United Kingdom, feels that, in the last decade, coaching has progressed from 'marginal to mainstream'.

People within organizations now discuss quite commonly the notion of 'coaching as a management tool', and write into their business plans that they are working towards achieving what they describe as a 'coaching culture', which recognizes the importance of intellectual capital in the race to keep ahead of the competition. Some organizations even admit to bringing in external coaches as a means of attracting and retaining staff;

they are seen as a company 'perk' alongside the gym, crèche and company car.

So, understandably, in this new era the demand for coaches is increasing daily. The Washington DC-based International Coach Federation currently boasts 3,200 members, more than double the figure of the previous year, and the UK-based Life Coaching Academy, which only opened in 1999, already has some 300 coaches on its books.

Even the traditional 'sitting by Nellie' style of coaching, which catered purely for acquisition of work-related skills, has been given a makeover and replaced with a huge range of tailor-made solutions to fit individuals' diverse needs. Cornerstone Consulting, a coaching organization operating in the United States, offers the following list as an illustration of the specific types of coaching now on offer within organizations:

- *Networking and career path coaching* – the championing of a specific individual, normally at a senior level.
- *Organizational and cultural coaching* – learning about your organization, its culture, vision, history and status in today's world.
- *Skills-based coaching* – helps employees to acquire knowledge and develop skills in order to carry out their job.
- *Team coaching* – the recognition of accomplishment as a team effort.

And for life outside the organization there exists an equally baffling list. Job titles such as 'sports coach', 'personal trainer', 'life coach', 'executive coach' – I even talked to someone the other day who told me she was a 'clutter coach' – have slipped, almost imperceptibly, into our business vocabulary.

THE PURPOSE AND BENEFITS OF COACHING

So, what has brought about this change in the way we perceive and use coaching as a learning methodology and style of management? What are its reported benefits for individuals and organizations? And does it work for everyone? There are a number of possible explanations and considerations, which are outlined below.

Coaching reflects the changing world of organizations

The stories that one used to hear in years gone by of people working for the same organization for a lifetime just don't happen in the 21st century. It is now more commonplace (almost expected in some cases) for employees to move from one company to another, or from one industry or profession to another, or even to set up in business on their own. Due to this shift in the job market, it would be naïve and impractical to expect one organization to take responsibility for *your* lifelong learning – a view very often held in the past. Instead, individuals are beginning to see themselves as just that – individuals – and recognize that if they want to be 'developed' then they have to play a more pro-active part in the process; they need to become more self-reliant and make a personal investment in themselves.

At a deeper level still, the onset of this new millennium seems to have prompted many people to start searching for more meaning and substance in their lives and in the work that they do. Employees at all levels are beginning to take a more holistic approach to their careers and their learning; to view work as being part of a bigger picture rather than something based purely around the acquisition of skills and bottom-line profits.

Books like Daniel Goleman's *Working with Emotional Intelligence* (1999), Charles Handy's *Beyond Certainty* (1995), and Stephen Covey's works on principle-centred leadership, have made leaders and managers all over the world re-examine their organizations and the people within them. They are beginning to realize that dealing with modern-day challenges and innovation now means managing such issues as trust, empowerment, intuition, and even 'spiritual intelligence'. Modern-day problems, issues and questions to be answered, as Charles Handy tells us, are not so much *convergent*, for example 'what is the shortest route to Bath?' which has only one correct answer, but more *divergent*, for example 'why do you want to go to Bath?' or even 'where do you want to go?', so the answers are endless!

All of which can be quite frightening stuff for those of us who were brought up on a cultural diet of 'do as I say, not as I do' and 'you're not paid to think'! Many coaches, particularly those working with senior executives, are being asked to guide and steer their protégés through these uncharted territories.

Coaching can be a cost-effective method of learning

Organizations are facing constant pressures to reduce costs, which very often means reducing the size of the workforce and cutting back on more traditional methods of learning, such as group training seminars. At the same time, these organizations are looking for a more highly capable, effective and flexible workforce, not just in terms of the acquisition of skills, but also in that less tangible range of concepts that we call 'personal development' – such things as interpersonal or human skills, goal setting, problem solving, creative thinking and so on.

Managers who once used to take an autocratic, didactic stance to leading teams of people, and trainers whose style of encouraging learning was of the 'jug and mug' approach, are both beginning to realize that by adopting more of a coaching style – that is, being aware of and supporting people's efforts, listening empathetically to the stories that evolve from those efforts, inspiring them by their own examples, and constructively challenging their assumptions – they can actually create a more positive and effective environment in which to work. Here, individuals are encouraged to take on more responsibility for their own learning and development, identify and solve their own problems and generally operate more efficiently and cost effectively.

Coaching helps to use people's capabilities

Some organizations are beginning to recognize that the skill and expertise they are searching for to pass onto the next generation might be under their very noses rather than lying in the heart of a huge external consultancy firm (see 'KNC Consulting' on p 167). Now, I'm certainly not criticizing external consultants – after all I am one myself – but my view is that the partnership that an organization would hope to have with an external consultant should enhance and not detract from the wealth of expertise that already exists within the workforce.

A survey carried out in the United States recently showed that more than *90 per cent* of employees polled felt that they had good ideas about the running of their organizations. But only *38 per cent* of them had actually volunteered their ideas, the majority of them stating that they felt their employers would not be interested in hearing them. Tapping into an employee's existing knowledge and encouraging them to share this knowledge for the advancement of themselves and the company, or 'knowledge management' to give it its modern label, is a very effective way of ensuring survival and growth as well as building that person's self-esteem and feelings of empowerment. Employees I meet and coach in organizations tell me that they love to have their personal worth recognized and valued – and that it happens all too infrequently.

On this topic, I heard Rosabeth Moss Kanter, an expert on managing change, tell the true story of a man working as a machine operator in a textile company in the United States. This company had a recurring problem with the quality of its yarn, which resulted in frequent yarn breakage and subsequent stoppage of machinery. The man, who had worked for the company for many years, had developed an idea to reduce the amount of yarn breakage. But it was only when a new chief executive officer arrived in the company, who took some time to walk round the factory floor and listen to some of the employees, that his idea was eventually voiced.

'What a wonderful idea – and so simple!' said the CEO. 'How long have you known about this?' he asked the operator.

'Thirty-two years,' came the reply.

Different learning methodologies suit different people

You're probably thinking, 'that's an obvious statement' and indeed it is, but I do think that those of us involved in education and training some-times forget it and tend to work with learning activities that we feel comfortable with, rather than considering the needs of the learners. Those of you who read my first book, *Tales for Trainers*, may remember the story of the young woman who was so scared of group training courses – and in particular her expectation of some of the traditional methodology such as role play – that she had to almost have her fingers surgically removed from the training room door! (There was a happy ending.) Was this young woman 'useless' because she didn't thrive in a group situa-tion? Was she 'under-performing'? Of course not – it was simply that group training was just not the best learning environment for her and she would probably have been much happier in a one-to-one coaching scenario.

Coaching can isolate and help correct unsatisfactory performance

If you are trying to diagnose and address some of the 'trickier' or more sensitive areas of an individual's performance – for example, interper-sonal skills, stress management, personal and professional goal setting, building self-esteem – coaching is often perceived to be a safer, suppor-tive and more confidential alternative to traditional group training.

My experience is that individuals are much more ready to admit to weaknesses, vulnerabilities or areas for development, and are much more receptive to working on those areas in a coaching environment than in front of their peers in a large group. In one-to-one coaching, egos, images and status can prove to be less of a barrier to learning.

A good coach can help to increase the coachee's awareness of such difficulties, engage them in positive narrative and guide them towards unlocking their own potential for problem solving. They can also provide useful feedback within a motivating environment, help to maintain or increase levels of self-esteem and empower them to take action.

Coaching can be more flexible than group training

Where organizations require a continual updating of skills, but also have to contend with the logistical problems of diverse geographical locations and varied working patterns, it is not always viable nor appropriate to address all these learning needs through large group training sessions.

A coaching session can offer an alternative learning environment and can be significantly easier to organize than a large group training day, particularly if the coach is taking advantage of some of the modern forms of communication open to them, which can reduce the need for class-room contact between tutor and learner. For example, many coaching sessions are now conducted over the telephone, via e-mail or using tele-conferencing.

Some group coaching is carried out via what is known as the 'TeleClass', where all those interested in a specific topic – anything from establishing life goals to improving your voice tone – ring into a central number and share their experience as a group online. A coach qualified in that particular subject facilitates the group session and gives feedback and follow-up activities.

However, I do believe that remote coaching of this sort will only work well if, at the outset, one establishes some 'ground rules' for the relation-ship, for example, the drawing up of a learning contract or personal development plan. A number of telephone coaches to whom I have spoken report that their coachees fail to telephone at the appointed time. For any coaching to work effectively, it has to be afforded the same weight and meaning as any other form of learning.

Along with the changing trends within organizations, the demarcation lines between work and home have – rightly or wrongly – become blurred over the last 10 years and the two are becoming more integrated. Domestic commitments, coupled with the advances in technology, have allowed more and more people to work from home, their daily routines and hours becoming more flexible. In line with this there is an expecta-tion that learning will be more accessible, and many coaches report that they allocate time (day or night) to fit in with their coachee's regimes. One external 'life coach' reports being on a '24 hour call-out' with his clients – for a price!

Coaching can teach you things the rule book can't!

Every company has its own set of rules and procedures, and we couldn't survive without them. Every company also has another 'under the counter' version, entitled 'The way we *really* do things round here', and it can be confusing – particularly for a new employee – to know when it is appropriate to follow which book. This is where organizational and cultural coaching can come into its own, particularly if carried out by a skilful coach, who is recognized as one of the select breed within the organization that anthropologist Peg Neuhauser (1993) calls 'the tribal elders' – those with many years experience, and many stories to tell. Warren Bennis (1996) says: 'Stories are more memorable and interesting than policy manuals and they seem to "empower". Tell a story and people will stop sleeping through your meetings.'

Too strict an adherence to the rule book can also disempower; if employees feel too restricted by fear of doing 'the wrong thing', their capacity for creativity and innovation is eventually killed off – and so are their stories! See 'Sticking to the Rules' (pp 152–53) for an example of what I mean.

The success of coaching

It has to be said that coaching as a learning methodology might not suit everyone or every situation. Like any learning method, one has to consider such elements as the pervading culture, the intended aims and objectives of the individual, their personality type, level of experience and their preferred learning style. However, coachees who have entered into this type of relationship for a period of time report great success and say that one-to-one coaching works for a number of reasons:

- The coachee's goals are kept uppermost in their mind, rather than being relegated to the habitual 'back burner'.
- Working together with a coach can greatly increase the coachee's creativity and motivation.
- Although it should be seen as a supportive partnership, a degree of accountability is built into a good coaching relationship, and coachees are required to take some sort of action towards achieving their own goals.
- Receiving good quality feedback and attention can dramatically improve the coachee's levels of self-esteem.

THE MODERN DAY COACH

So, has the job of a coach changed in the last ten years or so? At its most basic level, it might be said that the aims of coaching today are the same as they ever were, that is, to help others to grow and develop through enhancing their learning ability and their capability to function effectively.

Others argue that modern-day coaching goes much further than this. The International Coaching Centre in the United States says that a modern-day coach works together with a client *'to enable them to become more successful in all aspects of their life, by setting and achieving better goals, helping them to prioritize, constructively challenging and realizing their full potential'*. So modern coaching can take on a much more global aspect in its relationship with the coachee rather than being purely related to skills, and its focus is very much on two-way communication and building trust and rapport, rather than on telling and instructing.

Coaches can be required to deal with a great variety of situations and issues – they might be working one-to-one with a newly appointed director to help develop a new set of skills required at board level or helping an inexperienced entrepreneur create a business plan, but equally they could find themselves involved in group coaching with a team that is not performing well, or with an organization undergoing a period of change or restructuring.

In terms of the functional areas within which they operate, most of my colleague coaches (of all different breeds) with whom I consulted, identified the following as being the most frequently requested categories:

- **Envisioning and goal setting.** *'So what do you want to achieve?'* Establishing a clear picture of the future direction for work and/or life, setting specific goals – short- and long-term – to help achieve the aim.
- **Problem solving.** *'How are you going to achieve it?'* Acknowledging the existence and size of the problem, prioritizing problems, developing a range of practical and creative solutions, identifying barriers, considering suitability of options and identifying learning needs to solve the problem.
- **Reframing and creativity.** *'Let's look at this another way.'* Idea generation, encouraging lateral or creative thinking, seeing problems in a different, more positive way and finding ways of applying ideas.
- **Empowerment.** *'You can do it!'* Identifying what can and can't be controlled, encouraging self-reliance, taking responsibility for ones actions and identifying empowering or limiting beliefs.
- **Success and self-esteem.** *'I told you that you could do it!'* Finding ways of recognizing and rewarding success and building up healthy levels of self-esteem and confidence, particularly in dealing with difficult situations.

All of the above areas are concerned with change, transition, movement or transformation. Individuals work with coaches because they want to make certain changes and improvements in their lives and/or their work; they have a desire to move from where they are now to where they want to get to, and a coach can help them to decide on the destination, plan the journey and hopefully, arrive safely.

In order to give meaningful assistance and support on this journey, the modern-day coach requires certain skills and attributes. Eric Jensen (1988) says that a coach is 'more interested in providing direction in learning than the learning itself'. Marshall Cook in his book *Effective Coaching* (1999) says that a coach should epitomize such personal qualities as 'enthusiasm, trust, patience and respect' and demonstrate behaviour with their coachee which is focused and clear, knowledgeable, observant and goal-orientated.

Moreover, the very foundation of modern-day coaching has to be the command and use of exemplary communication skills, such as knowing how to give and receive constructive feedback, employing the most appropriate type of questioning, and demonstrating what Eric Parsloe and Monica Wray in their book *Coaching and Mentoring* (2000) call 'observant listening'. This means being aware that talking is only part of the communication process, and that most people demonstrate far more in their non-verbal communication, such as physiology, tone of voice, speech patterns and so on.

STORYTELLING AS A COACHING TOOL

So, where does storytelling fit into the coaching scenario? In two ways: firstly, there are the stories that they (the coachees) tell us, and secondly, there are the stories that we (the coaches) tell them.

The coachee's story

A good coach can elicit a great deal about coachees and their underlying thinking by encouraging and listening to the stories that they have to tell about themselves, and in particular the way in which they tell them. 'Narrative therapy', as it is called in psychological circles, has been used for many years by therapists to encourage clients to 'reframe' or see a problem situation differently. David Boje (1999) says that people can get on a track of telling the same (very often negative) story endlessly about themselves, which in turn can become a self-fulfilling prophecy. He says that employing this therapeutic method can help people to analyse and 're-author' the story and subsequently change their beliefs about themselves. David Boje says: 'Narrative therapy has to do with learning to tell a different story of yourself. Different stories are possible, even about the same events.'

Although coaching is not therapy, coaches working with employees in an organization can adopt a similar process. In fact, I usually find the majority of people love talking to a receptive listener about their jobs and what they do. In some industries and professions they even have a name for the process. When police officers in the United Kingdom tell nostalgic tales of yesteryear, they call it 'swinging the blue lamp', a flashback to the days when blue lamps were seen outside every police station.

However, we actually tend to shy away from or reject the negative, so-called 'yes, but...' stories that employees sometimes tell us, the tales whose opening lines usually revolve around the 'if only my manager would...', 'I wish customers wouldn't...', 'the company should...' type of language, and while I certainly don't advocate the use of gratuitous negative thinking and behaviour, there can actually be some validity in what psychologists now call 'defensive pessimism' or 'constructive negativity'. Some individuals are actually using stories like these as a form of self-preservation and to keep them in touch with reality. In addition, to be dismissive of these stories is to be unaware of the pervading or changing culture of an organization. Why go to the expense of commissioning an employee attitude survey when the information is all around you? Peg Neuhauser (1993) says: 'If you create an environment where people are afraid or not allowed to use that phrase (Yes, but...) you limit dramatically the amount of useful information that you will hear coming out of the organization.'

When you listen to the specific language that people use in telling their own stories, very often there is frequent use of metaphor (see Chapter 1). People tend to use metaphor (consciously or unconsciously) particularly when they feel some emotion – excitement, anger or happiness – about the topic they are speaking on and this is what brings the story to life. In fact, if you think back to the last boring speaker you heard, the chances are that he or she used no metaphor at all! Language without metaphor, imagery and colour is like the cake without the fruit.

Coachees describing themselves and their current and desired situation will very often talk in 'movement' or 'transition' terms; descriptions involving a journey, climbing a mountain, shooting for goal, playing a team game or fighting a battle are commonplace, and as coaches, paying attention to this type of language can tell us a lot about the coachee's underlying feelings.

The coach's story

As mentioned earlier, the very nature of coaching is to help a person identify and make changes and improvements in his or her life, and story-telling itself is very often known as a tool for self-transformation. If a story is perceived by the coachee to be metaphorical in nature, it can help them to draw a parallel between that and their own lives, to 'reframe' or see problems in a different light, and to be more receptive to change (see Chapter 1).

Many traditional fairy tales, myths and legends describe the hero or heroine going on a journey of some kind – whether physical, psychological or spiritual – from which, in spite of great adversity, they return home triumphant.

The philosopher Aristotle was quoted as saying that a good story encompassed 'the successful change from one status quo to another, to the emotional satisfaction of the user'. Joseph Campbell (1993) talks of the journeys of story heroes:

> A hero ventures forth from the world of common day into a region of supernatural wonder: fabulous forces are there encountered and a decisive victory is won: the hero comes back from this mysterious adventure with the power to bestow boons on his fellow man.
>
> (Campbell, 1993)

Storytelling, although a potent form of communication, is non-invasive as a coaching tool. People will respond much more readily to the gentle power of a story rather than a 'pull-your-socks-up' type of instruction, or probing questioning, which very often only breeds resistance in the recipient. In a coaching context, the coachee can be allowed to reflect on a story in their own way, and search for what the message means for them personally.

As discussed in Chapter 1, storytelling, although it is thought of as being primarily a right brain hemisphere activity, can actually encourage the joint working of both left and right hemispheres together, meaning that there is more opportunity for whole brain and creative thinking. This is why it can be inappropriate to give your one (and only) interpretation of the meaning of a story, because by doing so, you may be inadvertently activating the 'logical' left brain of the coachee, and forcing him or her to find a 'fit' with your interpretation. Better to allow the coachee's right brain the time to seek out its own pattern and a meaning that is relevant to him or her. The 'trigger' questions given for each story in Part Two of this book, if used appropriately, will still allow this process to happen.

So, how can storytelling be used specifically in a coaching context? In order to find the views and practices of other professional coaches working in the United Kingdom, I contacted the UK Coach List, a network of some 200 coaches (who can be contacted via e-mail at ukcoach-list@coachu.com) and e-mailed a questionnaire to its members. The questions I asked were intended to discover specifically:

- If and how coaches used storytelling as a coaching tool.
- What type(s) of story were used.
- What purpose storytelling was intended to serve.
- What effect(s) it had, if any, on the coachee.

Although it has to be said the response was quite small (around 30 in all), all the coaches who replied to my questionnaire (around 30 in all) reported that they used stories regularly in their coaching sessions. However, a small number said that they would not automatically use stories; it would depend on the appropriateness of the situation, whether they thought their telling a story was likely to distract the coachee, or if the coachee had their own example that they wanted to work on.

The most frequently-used types of story included *anecdote, metaphor* and *analogy*. A smaller number used *fairy tale, fables* and *myths/legends*. In addition, quite a few coaches said that they elicited more stories from the coachee than they told. One said that he encouraged his coachee to 'create a storyline of a situation' which they could then talk through and analyse together, and use as an ongoing frame of reference.

The most popular functional areas in which storytelling was used were *envisioning and goal setting, reframing a situation* and *building self-esteem*. A smaller number said that they used stories to help with such issues as *problem solving, empowerment* and *achieving success*. One coach told me that he used a story to 'get the coachee to fully see something they didn't want to see'. His feeling was that using a story was 'a gentle, less confronting way of dealing with it'.

When asked what their intended purpose of using stories was, the majority said it was to *stimulate thinking, to help understanding* and *to effect change*, with a smaller number saying that their purpose was to *motivate the coachee into action, to add humour* and *to entertain*. One coach reported that she used them to 'reach the unconscious' of the coachee, as a way of bringing unconscious thoughts into consciousness. Another coach told me that he encouraged his coachees to 'put things into context' and that using stories helped him to do that.

The majority of coaches reported that they *paraphrased* stories during the coaching session, with a smaller number saying that they took advantage of *e-mail, telephone,* or sent out *written material* to the coachee for them to study privately.

When asked what effect the stories had on the coachee, the most widely held view was that they *reinforced learning,* and in addition, the majority of the coaches said that stories *made people think,* they *helped people remember* and that they *moved people or stirred their emotions*. A smaller percentage felt that some stories could actually *change people's values and beliefs*.

The vast majority of the coaches who replied to my questionnaire said that, although they used storytelling very regularly in their coaching sessions, they felt that stories and metaphors could be employed even more; indeed one told me that, discussing it made him realize that he probably used them without knowing! However, all agreed that there was a danger in telling too many tales. One coach said, 'The coachee can become overwhelmed and then you lose the impact you hoped to achieve.'

CHAPTER 3

Finding and Using Stories in Coaching

FINDING STORIES

Many people have said to me that when it comes to the process of collecting stories 'it's easy for you; things *happen* to you!' I don't quite know what they mean by that, but it sounds as though they believe my daily routines of working, shopping, driving and eating are littered with wizards, trolls and sleeping princesses, and that there are dragons lurking in the dark recesses of my garden (mind you, bearing in mind the length of my grass at the moment, the latter notion is quite possible).

There is no magic formula involved in finding suitable stories to be used in coaching – they are everywhere! You simply have to tune your brain in to the 'story wavelength', so to speak. In other words, as part of your daily routine, keep your mind open to the possibility of useful material. In the meantime, here are a few ideas for sources that you might want to explore.

Personal experiences

American humorist James Thurber once said, 'Let us not look back in anger, nor forward in fear, but around in awareness.' You will see from Part Two of this book that many of the contemporary stories were born out of very commonplace situations. Over the years I suppose that I have developed a way of almost constantly assessing situations for their 'story potential' in a style not dissimilar to Kolb's learning cycle (1984). Kolb said that learning took place when any event or experience was followed by a period of reflection and then a generalizing or theorizing about future events. When assessing situations for their story potential, I ask myself questions such as:

● What happened in that situation?

- Who was involved? Did they remind me of anyone? In what way?
- Why did the event strike me as significant?
- What lesson(s) did I learn from that incident, and what underlying principles or patterns of behaviour were there?
- What parallel could I draw between this and the business world?
- Which of my coachees might benefit from hearing that story, and why?
- How could I help them to establish the link with their own lives?
- What change might this story bring about in this person?
- Is it appropriate and suitable for this individual/organization's ethics, values and so forth?
- Does it convey a positive/constructive message?

As a good coach you will always be on the lookout for useful material that any one of your coachees could use, and this process is just an extension of that. Many coaches and trainers tell me that 'the story finds them' and I think that can be quite true. It's amazing how often a situation presents itself to you that will coincide exactly with a problem you happen to be working on at the time. Or maybe it isn't so amazing. Psychologists would argue that it was just that part of your brain that seeks out pattern and recognition working overtime.

A very simple example of 'story potential' happened to me the other day. I was watering a plant in my conservatory, which I'm sorry to say had been badly neglected for quite some time and was looking distinctly droopy and sad (let's face it, it was dying!), and I was amazed how, the next time I looked at it, just about an hour after watering, it had miraculously perked up and was looking shiny and healthy again, just as if it had always looked this way! This made me start to think about the nurturing of human beings – whether in our personal or business lives – and how, although here too there can be serious cases of ill treatment and neglect, there is still the capacity to grow and blossom in the same way as my plant, with just the minimum amount of care and attention. And think of the additional heights that might be scaled through regular maintenance!

Another example tells the story of a colleague and dear friend of mine who had been working with me on designing a training workshop for an organization in the financial services sector. He sent me a copy of some handouts that he proposed to use and, although they were well thought out, and perfectly competently written, they seemed to me to be a little lacking in 'design flair', if you know what I mean. I personally set to with a will, adding clip art here, a 'think' box there and some clever headers and footers. By the time I had finished, they were completely unrecognizable. It was only when I saw my friend's dismayed face, that I was suddenly reminded of the story of the film *Mermaids*, which featured Cher in the starring role. She plays the eccentric mother, Mrs Flax, who, much to her sensitive daughter's chagrin, insists on taking the ordinary, man-sized sandwiches that her daughter has just made to impress her new boyfriend, and attacking them with star and diamond biscuit cutters in order to make them look 'dainty'. I shared the story – and the humour – with my friend, and the fact that I could now empathize better with his feelings of disappointment. Not only was a new training term invented between us that day (originally 'Mrs Flax handouts' and, more recently, 'Flaximized') which we regularly use, but also I have learnt never to touch his – or anybody else's – handouts!

It is when you reflect on a story such as this, and discover the *underlying lessons and principles*, that you can decide if the material is 'transferable', in other words – is it worth retelling to other people in the hope that they can glean the same or similar lesson to you? This I think is the crucial difference between carefully choosing and telling a story that is meaningful and effective, and churning out just one more of those unconvincing 'a funny thing happened to me...' tales that (a) usually never did happen; and (b) are never funny! The lessons and principles that I learnt from the 'Mrs Flax' example cited above were:

● I needed to be able to appreciate different people's 'maps of the world' (although an external situation looks the same, people have different perceptions of it depending on their internal frame of reference).
● I needed to demonstrate that I trust and respect the other person.
● I learnt that everyone has a different way of working – and that mine wasn't necessarily the best!
● I learnt that it was important for this person to be empowered to do things in his own way.
● I needed to focus on the intended outcome as being the important issue, and not attach too much emphasis on the method of achievement.

When you're using your 'story filters' to dredge through your own personal history, don't just choose success stories to retell. Coaches and trainers who, through the stories they tell, convey themselves as being the all-powerful, guruesque, superhuman types, apparently leading a perfect and blameless life, are not that easy to relate to or indeed learn from. I've seen quite a few coaches and trainers get into the 'and here's *another* story illustrating how wonderful I am' routine, which just serves to alienate them from their listeners. My experience shows that people endear themselves much more readily to you if you confess to some of your failures, mistakes, weaknesses and vulnerabilities – after all, you are human, just like them!

One of my own 'human' tales that I regularly tell to learners in the art of presentation is about how, some years ago, I was attempting to be a rather pristine 'Ms Perfect' on a presentation skills training course. Half way through the proceedings, and in front of a very quiet and, up until then, somewhat subdued audience, I managed to fall over the flip chart leg, knocking the whole thing spectacularly to the ground. (Come on, we've all done it...) With gritted teeth I muttered angrily, but as I thought imperceptibly, 'oh bum!', completely forgetting for the moment that the lapel microphone I was wearing was still turned on. But rather than being banished from the room as a complete failure, which was what I was anticipating, and losing all my credibility into the bargain, I was amazed to be greeted instead by spontaneous applause – and the level of rapport between the audience and myself rose almost palpably.

Why do I tell this type of story against myself? Because from my experience, most people – for whom the mere *idea* of giving a presentation can bring on a panic attack – can relate to it, they take heart from it and they can assimilate the learning into their own business lives. The typical messages that people tell me they derive from the above story include:

- professional speakers are not superhuman;
- things can go wrong – and it's not the end of the world;
- showing fallibility can sometimes increase rapport and credibility;
- shared humour is a great 'leveller' and rapport builder.

Friends and family

Everyone, it is said, has a tale to tell, and you will find that many people within your friends and family circle, with a little bit of encouragement, will be willing to share theirs. It's always worth either tape recording or writing these family stories down, so that they are not lost. I certainly regret the fact that I didn't transcribe more of my family stories – both my mother and father are now dead – and both were very good raconteurs. Peg Neuhauser, in her book *Corporate Legends and Lore*, tells the tale of her grandfather and what in her family became known as 'The Grand Canyon Story'. She says: 'You know that a story has real significance in your family if it has been given a name' (Neuhauser, 1993). Every family has at least one story similar to this tucked away in its oral history and it can serve a useful purpose by becoming an exclusive joke to be shared and enjoyed between the members, a shorthand language to describe certain situations – for example, 'it was a real *Grand Canyon* event' (after which everyone nods knowingly) or at a deeper level, a meaningful metaphor to increase understanding. Family stories are worth preserving and using with your coachees where appropriate, as most people can relate to a family situation.

But do be careful of any story content that they may prove sensitive to your coachee, for example, a few months ago, I nearly told a story about two young boys to a small group that included a man who had recently lost his young son through illness, but fortunately I realized the inappropriateness and stopped myself in time.

Also, be careful not to overdo your family tales. I attended a training workshop a while ago where the trainer only told stories about situations involving his wife. It was obviously a subject on which he considered himself an expert! Although it could be argued that there was nothing wrong with the story content, it was just a rather limited and one-dimensional approach – unnecessary when there is such a wealth of rich and varied material out there to be used.

Films and television

It is quite natural and easy to talk about the latest film release or television programme during a coaching session, and most people find it easy to relate to this. Be careful to choose positive or at least constructive tales; the majority of stories featured these days on news programmes tend to focus on the sensational and very often negative aspects of life. Stories should be there to uplift, or at the very least, to make people think; their aim is not to depress. Choose films with a strong storyline, and those with a useful and relevant pattern or analogy that you can match to a particular coachee's needs. Don't talk about a film just because you like it, and even worse, don't bore your listener to tears with your 'I've seen this film so often, I know it off by heart' rendition.

Fables

Most people have heard of the fables of Aesop and La Fontaine and, although they were written thousands of years ago, their messages are still relevant and just as fresh and 'punchy' today as they were then. Indeed, many of our most commonly used phrases and metaphors can claim their origins from fables, for example, 'The Tortoise and the Hare', 'The Fox and the Sour Grapes', 'The Boy who Cried Wolf' and so on. These are all easily accessible from bookshops and libraries – search both in children's and in folklore sections. The main library classifications that you will find useful are:

- religious myths;
- storytelling in education;
- mythology and folklore;
- storytelling (literature).

There are also a number of special collections of stories, for example, The Folklore Society Library in London, The School of Scottish Studies and The Ulster-American Folk Park Library. The addresses for these and others can be found at the back of this book.

Folk and fairy tales

Those of you who have children will no doubt appreciate the vast number of stories that exist in this category from all cultures around the world. As well as their entertainment value, many fairy tales hide a learning message that can be both contemporary (for example, 'The Ugly Duckling' is a classic tale of how to deal with low self-esteem) and complex (for example, 'The Sleeping Beauty' can offer coachees a way of dealing with and confronting a 'sleeping' or dormant aspect within themselves that they have been avoiding).

Myths and legends

Many of our everyday sayings have been extracted from this rich source of ancient stories, for example 'Pandora's box', 'Achilles' heel', and 'the Midas touch'. These all form a powerful type of shorthand language that can be shared with others to describe certain events or problem scenarios. It is worth listening to yourself (and others) to see just how many of the metaphors that are used originate from myths.

Mythological stories tend to be longer to read and sometimes more complex in content. This doesn't mean that they're not worth using as part of your coaching toolkit, it just means that you may need to put more work into your preparation before using them.

The Internet

Although some storytelling purists feel that technology is an unnecessary and almost intrusive newcomer to their art, it cannot be denied that there are a growing number of storytelling organizations and enthusiasts that have Web sites on the Internet, mainly, it would appear, in the United Kingdom, the United States and Australia (see the back of the book for addresses). Moreover, the term 'digital storytelling' seems to be slipping into our modern-day vocabulary. Dana Atchley, founder of the Digital Storytelling Festival in the United States – who uses the tool to help companies establish what he calls 'emotional brand-building' – defines the term as 'the art of using computers to create media-rich stories, and the Internet to share them.' You can see some of their digital offerings on www.nextexit.com.

Newspapers

Although very often filled with what I would call 'doom and gloom' stories, just occasionally, you might pick up a more positive or at least a moral tale that you can share with your coachee. And most newspapers are a good source of cautionary stories (just like Chaucer's *Canterbury Tales* in the 14th century) – examples of human intransigence, violence, ignorance and greed crop up everywhere (sadly).

Other coachees or clients

I very often find myself saying 'That reminds me of someone else who...' and this can be a very good source of stories, particularly as they are normally easy to relate to. Pat Williams, who uses storytelling as a thera-peutic tool, says in her workshops, 'How one person emerges from a difficult situation can often usefully be told to another individual in a similar situation.' However, be careful not to make the assumption that, because a particular type of intervention worked for one, it will work for all. This treatment will just give your coachee the feeling of being stereo-typed or boxed – and maybe even a failure, if it doesn't have a positive effect on them (see the story 'It's Easy', in Part Two). You also need to bear in mind the issue of confidentiality when using others' stories. You don't want your coachee thinking 'I wonder if they tell my story to other people?'

Whatever your source for choosing stories, it is worthwhile, whenever you come across one that gives you an 'aha!' – that is, it stirs your emotions, amuses you, intrigues you or just makes you think, to get into the habit of making a note of it somewhere, with a view to eventually building your own portfolio. From my experience, if you don't commit them to paper (or screen) somewhere – you'll forget them.

USING STORYTELLING ACTIVITIES IN COACHING

Having found your story, how are you going to use it? There is a vast potential for using the whole range of stories, metaphors, analogies and myths before, during and after a coaching situation and, like Joseph's amazing coat, they can be used in a rich, colourful variety of ways. The following activities are by no means exhaustive, but they are a selection of those with which I have personally had most success and that receive the most positive feedback from coachees. Feel free to use and adapt them for your own situation and purpose.

Before or inbetween the coaching session

One way of incorporating stories is to encourage learners to read and study a particular story or passage prior to, or inbetween, a coaching event. In this way, they can study at their own pace and reflect on the meanings of the text and what parallels might be drawn between that and their own lives.

One benefit of this method is that you are maximizing the time you have together – coaching sessions are typically no more than one to two hours in duration – and you are already working towards a mutual topic.

The writer and broadcaster Charles Handy is well-known for encouraging managers to use literature and the arts as a stimulating metaphor to contemplate. Stanford University in the United States has for some time been using Shakespeare's work as a powerful learning tool in its management development programmes. Cranfield Management School in the United Kingdom has gone one step further and collaborated with the Globe Theatre on London's South Bank to use some of the Bard's works to enhance its teaching on leadership, emotional intelligence and managing change. Cranfield director Leo Murray says that the metaphor of the theatre is 'a striking means of improving managerial and organizational performance'. Some examples of stories in Part Two of this book that work particularly well for private reading would be:

- 'The Wise Fisherman' (p 79);
- 'KNC Consulting' (p 167);
- 'The Prophet – on Talking' (p 100);
- 'The Spider' (p 84);
- 'In Which Pooh and Piglet Go Hunting' (p 88).

At the beginning of the session

Telling stories can be a light-hearted, non-invasive way of starting a one-to-one or group coaching session, rather than formal introductions. But make no mistake about the depth of some of these activities. Although some are humorous in content, they can also be very revealing in terms of people's identities and beliefs. This is a selection of 'story openers and introductions' that I have used.

Introductions – number 1: 'your favourite story'

This simple activity can be used either with a partner, if you are working with a small group, or simply as a stimulating discussion trigger if you are in a one-to-one coaching session.

Firstly, working with a partner/coachee, discuss what stories you remember from your childhood – they might be fairy tales, action stories, stories from pantomime, stories from comics or magazines, traditional tales or fables.

Secondly, having identified your favourite stories, is there a common pattern that emerges? What values do they embody for you? It might be courage, honesty, respect, curiosity or a sense of adventure. In what way do you still espouse these values today?

Introductions – number 2: 'company story'

This activity works best with small groups. I have found this a very useful way of beginning a training workshop, if I am going to be working with the group for some time. It works particularly well if you have a group mix of new starters to the organization and some of its 'tribal elders' that we mentioned earlier in the chapter.

Firstly, ask the group to discuss and then present 'The Story of Your Company and My Part in its Success'. This can be a very creative, participative and energetic way of getting a group to consider its history and origins and, because it is primarily a 'right brain' activity, you will find out more of the myths, legends and fables of that organization than you ever would from a sterile attitude survey! It is also a good way of encouraging individuals to consider how they fit into the 'bigger picture' or context – it brings an organizational chart to life.

Secondly, you can follow this up with a session on the organization's future, for example discussion on vision and mission statements, and so forth. You can guarantee that the group will be far less knowledgeable and confident here than they were in the last exercise, from which you can draw the conclusion, 'So, you have just spent [one or two hours] talking about your company's past – but you're not sure where it's going...' This gives a powerful parallel for the group to reflect on.

Introductions – number 3: 'metaphor cards'

This simple activity works equally well with individuals or groups. Its purpose is to have people consider and reflect on their own personal identity, or that of their team, customer or organization. I use a selection of metaphor cards that I give out to each individual or group. They contain a number of different questions such as:

- If you were an animal, what would you be?
- If you were a flower, what would you be?
- How is your job like a [everyday object] telephone/bicycle/ladder?
- If your team was a circus, what 'act' would each function be?
- If your organization was a pantomime/play/film, what would it be and who would play which character?
- If your organization was a football/baseball/cricket team, which would it be and who would play each position?

You will always find that some people relate to this type of activity more easily than others. For those who find it less easy, I encourage them to expand on their reasons for choice, which in turn is telling you more about them. For example, if you're working with 'How is your job like a ladder?' you can ask 'trigger' questions such as:

- What is the wall that you are leaning against in your job?
- What constitutes the rungs of the ladder?
- What happens when you get to the top?
- Is the ladder safe?
- Does it require anyone to hold the ladder? If so, who might that be?

During the session

Stories can be incorporated at various points during a coaching session. As well as the spontaneous and constructive storytelling that I hope both you and your coachee will indulge in, the following are a selection of more structured activities that you might like to try out.

Meditation/visualization

One of the original ways of working on a story was to meditate on it (see Chapter 1). In ancient Hindu traditions particularly, this was the way that one might be treated for depression and other personal problems. The story created a metaphor, a bridge from the fantasy world to the reality of your own life, and reflecting on it hopefully provided you with optimism and maybe some more creative ways of dealing with the problem.

If you are going to encourage your coachee to meditate, first be very careful that the story you choose is an appropriate one. The message that will go into the unconscious mind should be a positive and helpful one.

44

The way to meditate on a story, having read it through a few times, is to use the following steps:

1. Sit comfortably, either on a straight-backed chair or on a cushion on the floor. Keep your back straight but relaxed. This is to allow energy to flow through your body. Either close your eyes or lightly rest them.
2. Become aware of your breathing. Don't force it or do anything different than you normally would, just be more focused on the inhalation and exhalation, and visualize the air entering your nostrils and circulating through your body. Do this for approximately two or three minutes, until your mind starts to feel more still and peaceful. Any time your mind wanders (which it will!) bring it gently back to concentrating on your breathing. It may help to count the breaths, and see if you can reach seven without your mind wandering.
3. Gently remind yourself of the story text that you have just read. Let the message of the story and what it means to you float into your mind.
4. When you have achieved an understanding of the message, focus your mind single-pointedly on this for around two or three minutes. Again, if your mind wanders, remind yourself of the words of the story, and the message.
5. When you are ready, slowly open your eyes and bring your consciousness back into the room.

I have used this type of meditation technique with a small group, on a one-to-one basis, and also by asking the coachees to meditate on their own. Each one I found can be equally successful; it depends very much on the individual, and what outcome you are trying to achieve. Some examples of stories that work particularly well in this category would be:

- 'The Star Thrower' (p 77);
- 'The Prophet – on Talking' (p 100);
- 'The Hidden Gold' (p 178);
- 'A Final Note' (p 186).

Reframing activity

This activity can work equally well one-to-one or with small groups. If you are working with a small group, have groups of three people – coachee, coach and observer.

1. Coachees identify a problem or issue that they are currently facing, and describe it to the coach.

2. The coach listens to the problem and then offers the coachee a metaphor that describes it and makes a connection, for example, 'If this problem or issue were a journey, what type of journey would it be?' or 'How is this problem or issue like... [an animal, bird, flower, house and so forth]?' or 'If this problem or issue were like a story, what type of story would it be?'
3. The coach, working with the coachee, then extends the metaphor in some way – for example, 'So, what would happen if you took a different route?' or 'On this journey, are you travelling on foot or in a car?' The purpose of doing this is so that coachees can see their problems or issues from a different point of view, and to offer them more creative options and alternatives for dealing with them.

If the thought of coming up with a metaphor like that worries you, it may help to create a list of story words – for example, *king, queen, dragon, castle, forest, spells, magic, wizard, unicorn, prince* and so forth, to start you off. A word of advice: it is useful to first of all ask the coachee what type of metaphor or story he or she prefers. An example of this involves a woman I worked with some time ago who wanted to develop her business and was concerned that her potential clients seemed to be disappearing rather than accumulating. She had a particular liking for detective stories. I made up and told her the story of 'Sherlock Holmes and The Missing Clients'.

Another important point is that, although I personally thought that my first attempt at making up a story on the spot was a pretty amateurish affair and apologized profusely at the end, to my surprise my coachee loved it and said that it had given her a great new perspective on the situation. So, the point is, any story or metaphor that you use doesn't have to make sense to you – the important thing is, if it makes sense to your coachee – *congratulations!* You've done a good job.

A not-so-successful example of this technique happened to me when I was working in Europe not that long ago with a small group of managers from the media world. One Polish man in the group wanted to discuss his current position within his organization and I was trying to get him to relate his job to an act in the circus. He started to become anxious and visibly upset during this activity and, assuming that it was the thought of his current situation that was causing him distress, I offered consolation. 'But, no, you don't understand,' he said in broken English, 'I don't like *circuses!*' Let that be a lesson to you in the danger of making assumptions!

Your focus is to identify the pattern of the coachee's problem and to make a story around that. For example, a client of mine recently told me how worried she was about her teenage daughter who was going through a very difficult phase – not wanting to go out, having no friends, and generally feeling very low in self-esteem. I volunteered that she seemed to be going through an 'ugly duckling' phase (see Part Two for the full story). The client could immediately relate to this and together we recounted the story's happy ending. She later told me that she had reminded her daughter of the story – with positive effects.

Case study/discussion

All sorts of stories, anecdotes and metaphors, formal or informal, can be used for individuals or groups to read, listen to and reflect on. It is important, as mentioned earlier in this chapter, to work with the coachee to draw out the learning message or moral and to establish the links with their own experience. I'm often asked whether you should tell your coachee a story from your experience or rather attempt to draw one from theirs. Executive coach Steve Warren of Aquilegia Consultancy says:

> If I want to use an anecdote from my own personal experience, I ask the coachee's permission. For example, Barbara, a coachee of mine, is a very proficient horsewoman. Now, I know nothing about horses! However, I do know quite a bit about golf. The commonality that I refer to is the level of expertise that we both have in the two sports, not the sport itself. And that I find is something that Barbara can relate to very easily.

Some examples of stories that work particularly well for case study and discussion would be:

- 'Let There be Light' (p 82);
- 'Arrows' (p 86);
- 'Midas and the Golden Touch' (p 73);
- 'Two Caterpillars' (p 132);
- 'Alice and the Croquet Ground' (p 111).

Stories with humour

Although stories don't always have to be highly amusing or have a clever punchline at the end, humour is, after all, a very potent, positive and enjoyable emotion and when used appropriately (that means that everyone laughs – not just you) can aid the memory and learning process and can create a positive emotional climate for working with your coachee (see Chapter 1). Some examples of stories that work particularly well in this category would be:

- 'The Ignorant Thief' (p 93);
- 'It's Easy'! (p 104);
- 'Changing Course' (p 133);
- 'Not Ham Again!' (p 143).

At the end of the session

Stories can work very well at the end of a coaching session, to achieve 'wholeness' and completion, particularly if they are part of a 'running' story that you have started earlier on. A story can work well to reiterate the main learning points of the session (or the day if you have been running a group workshop) and to reinforce the principles and values that you may have been espousing. Stories can also help to clarify any confusion in learning that may have built up along the way. Some examples of stories that work particularly well in this category would be:

- 'The Devil's Toolbox' (p 109);
- 'The Grand Canyon Story' (p 121);
- 'The Choice is Yours' (p 145);
- 'Walls' (p 161).

Action planning

I have used a story format quite successfully as a form of action plan, rather than the more traditional, left-brain orientated version. This activity can work equally well with individuals – in which case you talk it through with them – or in pairs if you're working with a group. The types of questions I use are as follows:

- What is the 'pot of gold' you/your team is searching for?
- How would you describe the journey that you/your team will take towards the pot of gold?
- Who are the 'heroes' and 'villains' that might help or hinder you along the way?
- What are the most precious things you/your team will take on the journey?
- How will you know when you've found the pot of gold; what will you see, hear and feel?

I have found this to be a very powerful exercise that seems to help people to visualize the future for themselves and/or their team more easily. Some people report the journey to be a desert, a jungle, a motorway, an unmade path – there are endless variations! In addition, the content of this exercise can provide the coachee (and you) with some light-hearted sayings and useful shorthand phrases that you can both refer to in subsequent coaching sessions. For example, I am used to being told by my coachees 'we've met lots of villains this week!' and 'the jungle seems to be getting thicker!'

Chapter 4

Telling the Tale

'CRIC! CRAC!' – MAKING THE CONNECTION

Any manual that you care to read on professional storytelling will inform you that this is an interactive art, the success of which depends as much on the listener's part as on the teller's. American storyteller Barry McWilliams says that listeners' minds are 'the canvas on which the teller paints his tale' and that storytelling is a 'co-creative' process. The professional storyteller traditionally uses no visual images, props, costumes or stage sets, which means that listeners, in order to be involved and make sense of a story, have to create images for themselves in their own minds, based on the teller's performance and on their own experiences and beliefs. Storylistening is, therefore, an active rather than a passive activity.

This dynamic and inter-dependent relationship between storyteller and listener cannot exist without a mutual feeling of trust and rapport. And, with this in mind, the title of this section will be well known to all professional storytellers. The traditional cry of 'cric crac', which originates from the Caribbean, was used as a sign to an audience that a storytelling session was about to start. In order to gain their attention, the storyteller would shout 'cric!' to his audience, and wouldn't start telling the story until they responded with 'crac!' meaning that they were attentive and ready to listen. This ritual was the storyteller's way of making a connection with the audience, and extending an invitation to them to come along on the 'journey' of the story.

In more recent times, I have heard professional storytellers and speakers use variations on the same theme. One speaker I know says 'get it?' to his listeners, and expects to hear 'got it!' back. Others use noises, whistles or bells to herald the beginning of the story; some clap their hands; some light a candle. Some storytellers begin with a long pause – which can be just as powerful a cue.

Although you might argue that coaching is not a theatrical performance, and even if you're not too sure about the appropriateness of some of the more dramatic techniques like those just mentioned, the principle of asking permission to proceed, and obtaining some indication from your listener(s) that you have rapport is still a good one. You should always consider what process you will adopt for setting the scene for a story and testing the levels of trust and rapport between you and your listener. Storyteller Betty Rosen creates a shared and intimate atmosphere with her listeners at the start of a tale: 'I launched into this tale in the tone of voice of one in the throes of sharing secrets of juicy bits of gossip' (Rosen, 1988).

Without this rapport, it is certainly more difficult to persuade anyone into the relaxed and receptive state of the 'alpha' brain waves that we discussed in Chapter 1, and any outcome that you would hope to achieve from the storytelling may be limited.

I witnessed the opposite of this rapport-building process some time ago, when I was watching a trainer trying in vain to gain attention from a rather boisterous group at the end of a workshop. Visibly irritated, she shouted over the noise, using her best 'school ma'am' voice: 'Could I have your full attention for the story, *please*?' Although her listeners did eventually acquiesce and quieten, one felt that they were doing so rather unwillingly and that it was the 'sensible' left hemisphere of the brain that she had activated by her outburst rather than the more creative and playful right hemisphere. Storyteller Eileen Colwell advises: 'Storytelling is made of three essential elements, the story, the storyteller and the audience. Storytelling cannot be a success unless there is harmony between these three' (Colwell, 1980).

So, how do you achieve this state of rapport and synergy with your listener(s)? One of the fundamentals when you are planning on using stories for the purpose of enhancing learning, whether it be with individuals or small groups, is to achieve a balance between finding and telling a story that you like, and one that you think will also be appropriate and relevant for the listener(s). In my mind, both considerations are equally important. So, let's look at each perspective in turn.

THE STORYTELLER'S PERSPECTIVE

First of all, let's consider you. Whatever story you choose, it is important for you to feel – and appear – confident and convincing when telling it, and this will be difficult to do if you are unsure of yourself and your material. So, when deciding which story to use and how to use it, the following points can be of value:

- Decide on which category and method of story you would feel most comfortable using – will you tell a personal anecdote, retell someone else's anecdote, read straight from a text, paraphrase the text, use audio or video?
- Then – be your own audience! Read, listen and reflect on the story yourself, and notice your own reactions as you do so. Does it stir you? Make you think? Make you sad? Angry? Amused? Is the learning message obvious or obscure? Might there be more than one message?
- Consider how you are going to incorporate this story into your coaching session. Will you read it or tell it out loud, or will you ask your coachees to read and reflect on it in their own time?
- Some stories are great to read to yourself on the written page, but very difficult to read out loud – and vice versa. Personally, I think the only way you will know is to rehearse a story by speaking it out loud. The worst thing from a listener's perspective is to hear a storyteller stammering and stuttering; it ruins the 'flow' and can also interrupt the listeners' thought processes. They start to concentrate more on you and your delivery than on the content and message of the tale, and this is when the left hemisphere of the brain starts to 'kick in'.
- Visualize the story as you practise – the more vivid the better – and really try to bring the words to life in your own mind. Also, as you visualize, be aware of any sounds, smells, tastes and particularly any emotions that are also attached to the story. Remember that this was the way in which the original storytellers used to memorize their material, and it helped them to come across as more capable and compelling to their audiences.

Building confidence

When I run workshops on storytelling, I can always guarantee that at some point in the proceedings at least one of the course members will look at me anxiously and with disbelief, and say, 'But you can't do this with *adults*, surely?' to which my answer is always 'Why not?' But of course using this 'new' and innovative learning methodology (as some describe it) can be perceived as involving risk for the teller, and that's perfectly true – you never quite know how a story is going to be received.

But my answer to this is that if you're asking your coachee to cross new boundaries – for example, visualizing goals, imagining time-lines or role playing some future event – shouldn't you as the coach be prepared to take some risk too?

Some coaches and trainers confess to me that they would like to 'have a go' at storytelling, but say that they don't feel they have the necessary skills and are fearful of looking foolish or losing credibility. Those of you who remember the story 'Giant Steps' from my first book *Tales for Trainers*, will remember that the moral of the tale was that if you *take action and confront your fear head on*, eventually the fear will reduce in size, and who knows – it might even disappear altogether!

So, how are you going to take some 'giant steps' and build your confidence to deal with this perceived risk? Attempting to do this by simply giving yourself a sharp talking to, or administering an even sharper jot of gin, will probably produce short-lived or less-than-satisfactory results. The effects of working purely at behavioural level to build confidence are usually only temporary.

On the other hand, you might want to delve a bit deeper, and consider some of the possible limiting beliefs and values that you may have about yourself that might be holding you back. In Chapter 3 we discussed how you can use the power of metaphor to help your coachee in a learning situation, and this powerful technique can be applied just as effectively to yourself. When you make changes at the deeper levels of your thinking – in terms of your identity, beliefs and values – the effects will be longer lasting, and will in turn help you to strengthen your capabilities and shape your behaviour.

David Molden in his book *Managing with the Power of NLP* (1996) suggests that you challenge your own beliefs and values by identifying the key roles of your present job and then substituting a more illuminating and liberating metaphor. So, for example, rather than giving yourself a conventional role label such as coach, instructor or consultant, how would you feel if you thought of yourself as *a guardian angel, an entertainer, a shepherd* or *a grandfather*? Thinking of yourself in a more innovative way such as this encourages right brain thinking, which we know helps us to focus more creatively and flexibly, and makes us more receptive to change.

Another principle from the school of NLP that I have found effective in changing beliefs and building confidence is known as the act 'as if' frame, where you can examine and challenge your own beliefs by imagining a future event *as if* it were happening now. A favourite response of NLP-ers in answer to the habitual moan, 'But I can't do it!' is *'So, what would happen if you could?'* which is an option that some people may never have considered, or *'You can't do it – YET'* which implies that they WILL be able to do it some time in the near future. I find it amazing how these simple, yet effective manipulations of language can empower people, and how they can open up the possibility in people's minds of more creative and positive options.

So, the next time you are thinking of using storytelling as a learning tool, I invite you to act *as if* you had ultimate confidence in the content of your story, the outcome you want to achieve and in your ability to achieve it – and notice the differences that you or others might witness in your level of skill.

A frequent enemy of confident storytellers can be their own sometimes over-active left brain, which gets in the way and starts its 'reality check' takeover if they are telling a story. Occasionally I find that it sneaks its way into my consciousness, and whispers doubting messages in my ear, like, 'you can't do this; they're going to hate it.' You do need to be aware of any important verbal or non-verbal signals – positive or negative – that you might be picking up from your listener(s), but don't let this type of thinking sabotage your success. Although you can never totally eliminate a negative inner voice (and you probably wouldn't want to) you can at least reduce any harmful effects by saying positive affirming statements to yourself such as 'I am adding value,' or 'I am capable in what I do' and trust yourself that you are doing the right thing.

Integrity – whose story is it?

Remember the storytellers' vow that we mentioned in Chapter 1, which said that the content had to be *accurate, interesting and memorable*? Well you could do a lot worse than follow those principles. Particularly, don't pretend that something happened to you if it didn't. I have heard so many coaches, trainers and speakers do this, and it's very easy to see through it. If you are telling a tale that has been written or told by somebody else, then credit that person. There is certainly no harm in telling your listener(s) the origins of a story, there is no loss to the story content and in fact there is potentially a lot more to be gained in terms of your credibility and standing.

Congruence – are you an embodiment of the story?

Listeners will pick up as much or possibly more from who you are as they will from what you say. As an American speaker friend of mine says: 'Your life is your message.' Jo Radner, President of the American Folklore Society, tells us that 'the relationship between the teller to the story and the teller to the audience should be based on immense respect'. So, before you start telling a story in order to coach someone in good management practice for example, ask yourself: are you known for being the epitome of that practice? A story that extols the virtues of good customer care should only be told by those who embrace and demonstrate that philosophy themselves. We know that stories are immensely powerful and believable – but only if the teller backs up the story with his or her own actions. Otherwise, it becomes meaningless rhetoric.

THE LISTENER'S POINT OF VIEW

Our second consideration (but of equal importance) is the listener and how, through our storytelling, we can achieve rapport with that person. Nancy Mellon, professional storyteller in the United States, says that your 'intention is crucial' when you tell a story. You must always aim to have the highest intention on behalf of your listener(s). In other words, only use a story that you think will 'fit' with the person for whom it is intended, in terms of content, style, message and so on, and make sure that it matches their values, desired outcomes and personality style. When you are working with a group, you need to also consider the culture of the team or organization in which they operate. She goes on to say: 'A fiery person will not be impressed with a languid plot. Similarly, an excitable group that lives on high energy will not be calmed down easily' (Mellon, 1992).

There is nothing worse than being bored to death by people who *think* they are good storytellers (and there are a lot who do) telling you their favourite story – which has nothing to do with you and no bearing whatsoever on the situation at hand. This just gives your listener(s) the feeling of being manipulated and insulted.

Brian McDermott, from the Minneapolis training company Growthworks, whose business card reads 'Senior Partner' on one side, and 'Storyteller' on the other, says that 'stories without connection or context are deadly', and goes on to say that, in his presentations, although not all of his stories are his own, he certainly puts a lot of himself into his storytelling, and tries very hard to find and match stories with the needs of his audience.

'Canned' stories – that is, those you might buy randomly 'off the shelf' – chosen indiscriminately with no thought for the listener(s), or the adoption of a 'one-story-fits-all' policy, have little to offer as a means of learning. Only the other day I attended a meeting in a manufacturing company and one of the senior managers started telling a (very long) story about his early days in manufacturing. As we all walked into lunch, a junior manager whispered to me: 'I think he's only got one story; I've heard that one so often, I could tell it myself!'

Poor choice of stories can be one of the quickest ways for storytellers to lose rapport and credibility with their audience. To be a sensitive and effective storyteller you need to 'enter the reality' of the person for whom the story is intended. This means that you will need to make the journey into their world – to understand their thoughts, values, beliefs and learning objectives – rather than expect that they will come into yours. Chip Bell, in an article on storytelling, says that a story should be: 'Tailored to fit the storyteller, audience and learning objective. The objective is paramount. Stories without purpose obviously lack relevance, but they also tend to lack charm' (Bell, 1992).

Telling a story that is seen as being both appropriate and meaningful to the listener(s) can be not only a powerful learning experience but also a way of demonstrating your understanding of them, their world and their particular objectives. It is a great way to show respect and gain rapport!

Perceptions – do you really *know what it's like to be in their shoes?*

Although we might commonly say to a coachee 'I can put myself in your shoes' or 'I know how you feel' it is very rare that we actually mean it, unless we have gone through a similar experience to the one that they are describing – and even then, there's no guarantee that our perception of that situation would be identical to theirs. I sometimes actually say to a coachee, 'I don't know how you feel, but I'm trying very hard to understand.'

One of the ways in which you can improve your understanding and level of rapport with another person is to stop being you for a while, and actually imagine yourself being him or her, a technique known in NLP circles as 'perceptual positions'. This technique affords us an opportunity of seeing a situation from three different points of view. Here is an exercise that you can try out on your own, or work through with a colleague:

- Step 1: Imagine the time and place where you will be. Sit or stand where you will be telling the story. Imagine actually telling the story in your mind. Imagine the listeners and their reactions. From this position, what do you see, hear and feel? Be aware of any information you get from this position.
- Step 2: Now imagine being the listener. Actually sit or stand where your listener will be. Sit or stand using the same postures and gestures as your listener. Really think of yourself *as your listener* listening to the story. From this position, what do you see, hear and feel? What additional information does this give you?
- Step 3: Now imagine you are a fly on the wall. Imagine yourself telling the story and the listener listening. Imagine yourself and your listener interacting. From this position, what do you see, hear and feel? What advice could you give yourself to improve the situation?

Being able to imagine a situation from three different aspects gives you the flexibility to change certain elements of your behaviour in order to maintain or improve rapport with the listener. More information on this technique can be found in Joseph O'Connor and John Seymour's book *Introducing NLP* (see the References section at the back of this book).

Audience participation and involvement

However good a storyteller you might be, please don't get carried away with the sound of your own voice and think that you have the monopoly on good tales. As previously mentioned, storytelling is an interactive performance art and it is this very interaction that creates a bond and closeness between the teller and the listener. Ellen Munds, producer of Storytellers Theatre in Indianapolis, says that 'the audience is very involved in the process of the story, though they may not think about it... you walk away with a shared story.' You can encourage participation first of all by telling stories that your listener(s) can relate to and feel part of. There is no point your talking about 'the last time I flew out to the Far East' if your listeners have never been outside Bradford.

If you are working with a group, you can encourage the members to share their thoughts by asking rhetorical questions or using a 'call and response' type style, for example, 'What would you think happened?' This can be a powerful method because it makes people feel part of the story process; it engages their emotions and ultimately improves memory potential. However, it is risky! You must be prepared to get – and deal with – reactions and answers that you weren't expecting!

I have also used a running dialogue type approach (best used with a group) to encourage participation, where I choose one person in the group and hold a 'mock' conversation with them along these lines: 'Supposing Helen and I were talking about goal setting, and Helen says to me, "I don't have a clear idea of my future goals" then I might say to her...' Invariably, at some point, if you have been convincing, listeners become so involved and absorbed in the dialogue that they start to volunteer their own responses, usually without even realizing that they are doing it. Sam Cannarozzi, in an article written for the Storytelling Society, gives a charming example of this process. He observed an African woman storyteller, who told a tale of a young girl sent to fetch food for her grandmother. Turning to a little girl in the audience, she asked why the food hadn't arrived yet. The girl, totally engrossed, was on her feet and answering before she realized that it was simply a part of the story! This is a good example of the 'flow' effect mentioned in Chapter 1, and used skilfully, can be a wonderful and non-invasive alternative to role play!

If you are working on a one-to-one basis, you would expect your coachee's participation and involvement to be more natural and forthcoming; simply through skilful use of questioning and listening. Good coaches can always encourage and listen to their coachee's use of narrative. As discussed in Chapter 2, the coach needs to pay particular attention to type of language (verbal and non-verbal) that coachees use as this can reveal a great deal in terms of their underlying thinking.

In whatever context, individual or group, appropriately-used stories can encourage people to contribute and become involved without intimidating or embarrassing them.

TELLING THE STORY

Having done our preparation from our own and the listener's point of view, we now need to consider how to tell the tale. Now don't panic! I say that, because I do find that this is the part of the process that worries most people. They seem to think of all storytelling as being a particularly challenging form of presentation (and we all know how people feel about presentations) and, although that might be true if you were being judged as a professional storyteller in some formal context, it's not true when used as a learning methodology in the more relaxed context of coaching. You need to have in mind that storytelling is a joint effort between you, the story and the listener. Augusta Baker and Ellin Greene say:

> Storytelling is a sharing experience...when we tell, we show our willingness to be vulnerable...storytelling properly done, produces a relaxed, restful feeling. It establishes a happy relationship between teller and listener, drawing people close to one another...this rapport carries over into other areas as well.
>
> (Baker and Greene, 1977)

Your listeners don't expect a 10/10 performance but what they do expect, and these are some of most important elements that you need to weave into your delivery, are qualities such as sincerity, enthusiasm and credibility. The main way in which we can create these qualities is through the use of our own verbal and non-verbal communication.

Breathing

Obviously your personal style of storytelling will vary depending on the size of your audience. If you're talking to a small group, it is still something of a performance – albeit a low-key one – and this will be reflected in your use of voice. If you are working one-to-one then the style will be more natural and conversational. Either way, proper breathing is a good discipline for those who make their living from using their voice! And proper breathing only comes from practice and experience.

Someone once gave me the advice (and they were quite right) that it's impossible to perform breathing and other stress management exercises properly WHEN you are stressed. It's too late! I remember once listening to a stress-management tape, and was so stressed that I started 'fast forwarding' sections to save time! I was furious when it didn't work – until I realized how ridiculous I had been!

Any kind of breathing exercises are extremely effective for improving your speaking voice, but don't think that you can start doing them in the middle of working with your coachee or group of learners. If you're considering telling a story, particularly if you haven't used this method-ology before, you should start exercising, or at least become aware of your breathing, some two to three hours prior to the event. Patsy Rodenburg in her books *The Right to Speak* and *The Need for Words* gives some very good examples of breathing and voice exercises (see the References section at the back of this book).

Getting started

Just as we see some tennis players at Wimbledon ritually bounce the ball three times with their left hand, spin their racquet round twice anticlock-wise and wipe their foreheads with a favourite handkerchief, some story-tellers advocate 'psyching' themselves up in the same way. Well, not *quite* the same way, but some have a favourite stance or position in the room that they adopt to get themselves in the right frame of mind.

Although it might fly in the face of the presentation skills rule book, I sometimes, when telling a story to a group, prefer to stand with one foot crossed over the other and my arms loosely folded in front of me. Another storyteller reports starting each story by joining his hands behind his back and bending over at the waist as though searching the ground for something. While in this position, he thinks about what he wants the story to convey. As well as helping you to get in the right frame of mind to begin, it is also a good way of creating an 'anchor' for your listener. In other words, they begin to associate a particular stance or gesture with the commencement of a story. One woman in a small group that I worked with recently told me that she instinctively put down her workbook and pen when she saw me adopt 'that' pose, as she knew it was a time to relax and just let the information sink in.

Introductions and transitions

To become an accomplished storyteller, you will need to develop a range of 'openers' and 'transitions' to lead you into your story. Your aim should be to glide into a story seamlessly, rather than there being an ugly hiatus at the start. When choosing an opener or transition, do be careful of using the line 'let me tell you a story' every time, or indeed of repeatedly using any line. In the section above I talked about 'anchors' and it is just as possible (in fact it's sometimes more common) to have a negative anchor as a positive one. If you don't believe me, watch what happens the next time you say to a learner: 'And now, time for you to do your introduction/presentation/role play...'

Be observant of any reactions you get from your listener(s) in response to any opening line. If any phrase is greeted with a groan or equivalent non-verbal gesture, you know you've overdone it. And there is no need to be restricted to the same line for starting a story. You can choose from any of the following, or hopefully they might give you some ideas to adapt to your own style:

- I had a friend once who...
- I was reading the other day about...
- That reminds me of...
- I knew someone who...
- A friend of mine...
- Did you ever hear the story of...?
- Everyone knows...

Or more traditionally...

- Once upon a time...
- Far away and long ago...
- In a land that never was, in a time that could never be...
- In a place, neither near nor far, and a time, neither now nor then...

More story openers and introductions are available on the Internet. Doug Lipman, who describes himself as a storyteller, musician and coach, offers a number of excellent Web pages on this and other aspects of story-telling at www.storypower.com.

Voice

Although it has been said that the secret of being a good actor is the ability to tell a good story, happily I wouldn't say that the reverse is necessarily true. Some professional storytellers have, of course, studied acting, performance or other voice management skills, and although you may find these useful in order to boost your confidence, they certainly aren't a mandatory requirement in telling a story. In fact, using professional acting skills for the type of adult 'business storytelling' that we are discussing here can actually lead to your sounding too polished, too well-rehearsed and scripted, and thus unbelievable. In addition, if there is a huge gap in terms of the perceived difference between you and your listener(s), it makes it more difficult for them to relate to you and the story you are telling.

However, storytelling is an oral medium, so effective and appropriate use of the voice, and such qualities as *tone, pace, pitch, volume* and *emphasis* are of paramount importance in creating the right atmosphere. In addition, I believe that using your voice for business storytelling with adults in a business context requires a particular skill. The way you use your voice to start a story is crucial. This is your equivalent of 'cric! crac!' and where you gain (or lose) rapport very quickly. Try to match your voice tonalities as closely to your listener as you can. Listen for the type of words they use, the metaphors, the language patterns, the pace, volume and so on. If you are working with an individual, this is a fairly straightforward thing to do if you've been listening attentively; if you are working with a small group, you have to pick up the general 'feel' of their voices, the culture of the language and what is acceptable to them.

At the beginning of your story, have in your mind that, although enthusiastic, you are still grounded in reality and this will be reflected in your tone of voice. Even if you are using the age-old 'Once upon a time...' you can still use your normal, everyday business voice until you can tell that a bridge of trust has developed between you and your listeners. Once you have achieved that, and have your listeners 'hooked' so to speak, and it doesn't normally take long, then, and only then, you can take the pace and tone of your voice down a couple of notches, which will help them towards the 'alpha' brain waves and a more relaxed and receptive state.

The following checklist can be useful when preparing and rehearsing your voice for the delivery of your story.

- Be aware of the tone, pitch, pace, volume and colour in your own voice and match these as closely as possible to your audience. This is one way of gaining rapport with them.
- Modulate the tones of your voice to create interest, enthusiasm and involvement and to establish the mood you are trying to create – but don't over-dramatize.
- Don't use a 'kindergarten' voice. Your listeners will switch off quicker

than you can say 'once upon a time' if they think they are being patronized.

- Lower your voice tone and volume to create suspense and authority.
- Avoid nervous voice habits, such as 'er' and 'um'. Better to be silent than to lapse into these. Your listener(s) can lose confidence in your ability.
- Don't try to change your voice tones too often if there are different characters in your story. This can prove distracting for your listener(s) and can also be very difficult for you to maintain. It's easy to forget which voice belongs to which character!
- Repetition and exaggeration have always been fundamental elements in storytelling. Repetition of a phrase helps to build patterns and lock the thought into the listener(s) mind. Exaggeration encourages humour, which in turn relaxes listeners and makes them more receptive to your message.

Non-verbal communication

As coaches and trainers we know what an important role body language has to play in the overall communication 'package'. However, do keep in your mind that in business storytelling the main focus should be on the story and the underlying message. Any body language that you use should be simple and natural, and should always serve to enhance the story, not detract from it. Eileen Colwell says that 'storytelling should be restful to watch as well as to hear' and warns 'beware of exaggerated gestures, for they can easily look ludicrous' (Colwell, 1980).

Your use of non-verbal communication will, of course, vary depending on whether you are working with a group of people or an individual. When it's the former, you may well want to stand to deliver your tale, and it is quite appropriate here to use broader, more dramatic gestures and more movement. If you are working on a one-to-one basis, it would be more appropriate to sit, using slower, more calculated gestures.

The following checklist can be useful when preparing and rehearsing your non-verbal communication for the delivery of your story.

- Your facial expression should always be congruent with the tale you are telling. You will lose all credibility if you are supposedly telling a tale of woe with a big grin on your face! Where there is perceived incongruence, people will believe the visual rather than the verbal.
- Be aware of the importance of eye contact. Its purpose is twofold: first of all if you make regular (but not continuous) eye contact with people they will feel involved and will feel as if they are a part of what you are saying; secondly, you need eye contact to find out the

response from your listeners to what you're saying in order to make any necessary adjustments to your own behaviour.

● Gestures can add to the general dramatization and visualization of your story, but keep these to a minimum so that they don't detract from the message of the story, and so that any you do use are recognized as being significant.

● If you're working with a group, you can use closer proximity to the group to create suspense or drama, and to encourage participation where appropriate.

● Be aware of your posture. A slouching posture tells your listener(s) that you are indifferent to your own story. A good posture, as well as indicating confidence, encourages you to breathe and speak more effectively.

Closings and bridges

Just as important as the beginning of a story, you need to find a way to end it conclusively and positively. Happy endings to a story provide the listener with a feeling of closure or wholeness. As Nancy Mellon says, 'a happy ending is holy ... *and they lived happily ever after* is the equivalent of a triumphant finale' (Mellon, 1992). Unhappy endings, on the other hand, although by no means prohibited, do the opposite and leave the listener still pondering. As with the openings, there is no need to be restricted to using the same line every time. You might choose from the following:

● How about that for a real story!
● But that is another story.
● And that's a true story!
● There you have it.
● This is my tale.
● What do you think?
● That was just the beginning.

Or more traditionally...

● And they lived happily ever after... or if they didn't, it's none of our business.
● And this was a story of how it happened.
● The end.
● They lived happily ever after and were never bothered again.
● And now the story is yours.
● And that is how it is to this day.

As well as finding a suitable end, you should if you can, develop a transition or 'bridge' for your listener(s) from the story back into their own lives, for example:

> And so it's nearly time for us to finish...and you're maybe already thinking about going back to work later/tomorrow...and while you're pondering on the story...and thinking about what you have learned from it...you may find that the story has something to tell you about yourself and the job that you do...

And when you've come to the end of the story – STOP! Don't feel that you have to ramble on or explain what the story means. As stories work at different levels for different people, it is very often better for you to let your listeners reach their own conclusions.

And most importantly, don't be afraid of the silence that very often follows a storytelling. It's the most magical time! It's the time when your listener(s) are taking it all in, reflecting and pondering and very often making links between the message of your story and the story of their own lives. At this point, listener(s) can still be in a semi-trance state, so do be careful not to break that state with a 'SO – back to work!' rabble-rousing cry. And please don't do what a (not-so-skilled) colleague of mine used to do when working with a group. He would end his delivery with a resounding 'THANK YOU!' which, even if his listeners didn't feel like it, used to draw out a grudging and rather half-hearted ripple of applause.

So, instead, if the end of your story is followed by silence from your listener(s), just savour that silence with them, and let your voice resonate and linger in the air for a little while. Eileen Colwell says that 'the greatest tribute that can be paid to a story is the moment of silence that sometimes follows...the (listener) has been lost in another world and it takes a little time to return to the everyday. Let him have that interlude' (Colwell, 1980).

So, now that I've come to the end of this chapter, I shall stop, share with you an interlude of silence, and then, if you're sure you're sitting comfortably, I'd like to tell you a story...

PART TWO

Then I'll Begin...

How to Use the Tales

There are 50 tales in this anthology, ranging from two-minute anecdotes to 10-minute stories. Each story can be used just as effectively in a one-to-one coaching session, or as part of small group work. The 50 tales are categorized – 10 stories in each section – into the five main functional areas that coaches most commonly work on with their coachees. The following list is an overview of the specific areas of learning within each section.

ENVISIONING AND GOAL SETTING

'So, what do you want to achieve?'

The stories in this section can be used to discuss such aspects as:

- having a desirable and achievable vision;
- setting realistic goals;
- successful planning and prioritizing;
- working with others to achieve the goal;
- breaking a task down into small, achievable units;
- having the faith and confidence to start;
- making sure that the goal you *think* you want is actually what you do want;
- personal and team goal setting;
- styles of leadership to help you achieve the goal;
- practical ways to achieve the goal;
- positive goal setting, positive thinking.

PROBLEM SOLVING

'How are you going to achieve it'?

The stories in this section can be used to discuss such aspects as:

- creative and lateral thinking;
- the need to challenge 'the rules';
- the role of learning and coaching in problem solving;
- using experience to solve problems;
- viewing 'failure' as a natural part of the creative process;
- the dangers of 'self-fulfilling prophecy';
- how different people perceive and deal with problems;
- constructive problem solving;
- getting feedback in our problem solving;
- planning and prioritizing problems;
- paying attention to detail;
- having faith and determination;
- bringing problems down to size.

REFRAMING AND CREATIVITY

'Let's look at this another way.'

The stories in this section can be used to discuss such aspects as:

- flexible and creative thinking;
- taking a different vantage point to a situation;
- reframing an issue or problem;
- reframing your attitude to your goals;
- appreciating other people's 'maps of the world';
- not attempting to 'fix' people with one solution;
- realistic thinking;
- practical solutions;
- creativity in change management;
- changing paradigms.

EMPOWERMENT

'You can do it!'

The stories in this section can be used to discuss such aspects as:

- the real meaning of personal empowerment;
- taking responsibility for our own actions;
- believing in your own capabilities;
- creative and positive thinking;
- seeing things from a different perspective;
- not relying on other people to make decisions for us;
- leaders and teams and team empowerment;
- vision and creative thinking in empowerment;
- the effect of beliefs and values;
- freeing yourself from constraints – real or imaginary;
- the effect of rules and procedures on empowerment;
- taking risks.

SUCCESS AND SELF-ESTEEM

'I told you that you could do it!'

The stories in this section can be used to discuss such aspects as:

- building self-esteem;
- giving praise and reward;
- giving and receiving feedback;
- people's perceptions of others;
- building self-confidence;
- believing in your own capability;
- having courage in your own convictions;
- developing self-esteem through learning and understanding;
- being aware of your self-image and identity;
- goal-setting to achieve success;
- hidden talents, latent skills;
- achieving success – both individually and as a team;
- the power of positive thinking;
- influencing and assertiveness;
- personal achievement.

As with my first book, I have borrowed a formula from Aesop and each story page follows this structure:

- *Introduction* – the origins of the tale, in what circumstances I have used it, and so forth.
- *The tale* – the content of the story.
- *Moral* – the learning message of the story.
- *Reflection* – in what situations you might use the story, plus 'trigger' questions if you need them, to help the coachee to make the connection.

Although some storytellers would disagree, I think that you should decide whether you want to divulge the moral of the tale or leave it for your coachees to ponder on for themselves. It depends very much on the situation and the individuals concerned. If your main aim is for the story to just 'rattle around' in their subconscious for a while until they make their own meaning, then just tell the story and leave it at that. If, however, you want to use the story for a more specific purpose, to open up discussion, or for future action planning, then you might use some of the trigger questions listed to help the coachee draw a parallel between the story and their own situation. But do remember not to make the questions sound like a 'third degree' otherwise you will prompt the 'sensible' left brain into action!

In order to choose a story, consider first the aspect you want to discuss or explore in your coaching session, for example, you may be working with a coachee on the idea of *positive goal setting*. First look through the overview section for envisioning and goal setting on the previous page, to see whether that particular aspect of goal setting is covered. In this case, *positive goal setting, positive thinking* is listed. As some of the story topics overlap, it is worth skimming through the other sections, for example, in the success and self-esteem section, *setting goals to achieve success* is also listed.

Turn to the stories themselves, and flick through the 'introduction' and 'reflection' parts to see which tale would best fit your need. As with all good storytelling, feel free, when you're telling the tale, to adapt, shorten or elaborate with your own experiences or memories. The most important thing is for you and your listeners to enjoy them!

Envisioning and Goal Setting

'So, What Do You Want To Achieve?'

These stories encourage people to see their mission and goals clearly, to reflect on whether a goal is indeed theirs or somebody else's, to be specific in their goal setting – and most importantly, to consider what they will do if they achieve it.

1

INTRODUCTION

This story is so well-known that it has been incorporated in a figure of speech in our day-to-day lives. We use the term 'the golden touch' or 'the Midas touch' as a positive description of people who have won huge amounts of money in a competition, or who have been successful in their careers. But I think it is worth remembering the full story of Midas as told in the original Greek Myth...to remind ourselves of the possible danger involved in wishing for something and later regretting it.

THE TALE

Midas and the Golden Touch

Midas was the King of Phrygia. He was a very wealthy man – who wanted to be even wealthier. One day, whilst walking in his garden, he came across an old man lying on the ground fast asleep, apparently sleeping off the effects of too much wine. The man was called Silenius and he was a great friend and companion of Baccus, the god of wine and merriment. Midas smiled to himself when he recognized the man.

'Silenius must have been over-indulging again!' he said to himself.

Gently, he helped Silenius to his feet and made him welcome in his palace. Baccus, on hearing of Midas's kindness to his old friend, wanted to offer him a reward for looking after Silenius so well.

'I will grant you whatever you wish for,' Baccus told Midas.

Now Midas, being rather a foolish man, didn't wait to be asked again. He quickly told Baccus that he wished more than anything to have everything he touched turn to gold.

'If you're sure that's what you want,' said Baccus, knowing that Midas would live to regret his wish, 'consider it done.'

Midas could hardly wait to put his new skill to the test. He picked up a flower – and straightaway it turned into shining gold. Midas was beside himself with excitement. He touched a chair, a table, a vase – all of them turned into gold.

Overjoyed, Midas called his servants to prepare a huge banquet in celebration. But as soon as he raised the food to his lips – it too turned to gold, and was impossible for him to eat. Everything he touched – bread, fruit, meat, the same thing happened. He tried to drink some wine, but as soon as it touched his lips it turned to molten gold and stuck in his throat.

Midas fell to his knees and cried to Baccus for help. On hearing him,

Baccus, who was a kindly god, told Midas to go down to the river Pactolus and bathe in its waters. Midas did as he was told, and discovered to his relief, that not only had he lost his golden touch, but he had also lost all desire for gold and wealth. When he got out of the river, he saw that the sands had turned to gold.

MORAL

One can have too much of a good thing.

REFLECTION

You can use this tale to discuss issues such as having a desirable and achievable vision, and setting realistic goals.

What represents the 'gold' in your life or in your work?
What makes this goal so desirable to you?
Is this goal congruent with you and who you are?
What might you stand to lose when you've achieved the goal?
Will you still want this goal?
What will happen if you don't achieve the goal?
Could you set a more realistic or achievable goal?

2

INTRODUCTION

Everyone has heard of Aesop's fables. Like Homer, Aesop is a legendary figure, who may or may not have existed. History books tell us that he was a Greek slave living before the time of Christ. Over the years his stories have become synonymous with learning, wit and a common-sense approach to life. For a great many people, Aesop is still 'The Storyteller'.

THE TALE

Look Before You Leap

A fox tumbled into a water tank and couldn't get out. Eventually, along came a thirsty goat and, seeing the fox, asked him if the water was good. The fox jumped at the chance. He sang the praises of the water with all the eloquence at his command and urged the goat to come down. The goat was so thirsty that he went down without stopping to think and drank his fill. Then the two began to consider how they were to get up again.

'I have a good idea,' said the fox, 'that is, if you are willing to do something to help us both. Be so kind as to place your forefeet against the wall, and hold your horns straight up. Then I can nip up, and pull you up too.'

The goat was glad enough to comply. The fox clambered nimbly over his haunches, shoulders and horns, reached the edge of the tank, and began to make off. The goat complained that he had broken their pact. But the fox only came back to say, 'You have more hairs in your beard than brains in your head, my friend. Otherwise, you wouldn't have gone down into the tank without thinking how you were going to get up.'

(From *Fables of Aesop* translated by S A Handford, 1954, Penguin Classics. © S A Handford, 1954.)

MORAL

Never embark on an enterprise until you can see your way clear to the end of it.

REFLECTION

Use this story for discussing realistic goals, successful planning and prioritizing, and working with others to achieve goals.

In what way might you, or someone you know, be the fox or the goat?
How could the fox and the goat work together more collaboratively?
What represents the water tank that might lure unsuspecting people in?
Have you embarked on a project without envisaging its conclusion?
Who in your organization would help to pull you out of the water tank?
Who might you help in the same way?

3

INTRODUCTION

Loren Eisley, the American anthropologist, was the originator of this retold story. I have heard numerous speakers tell variations of it as part of their motivational talks, and I think it's a wonderful tale of encouragement for people who are on the point of giving up – and haven't we all felt like that at some point?

THE TALE

The Star Thrower

A man was walking along the beach when he noticed a young boy apparently picking something off the ground and throwing it out into the sea. As the man got closer to the boy he saw that the objects were starfish. And the boy was surrounded by them. For miles and miles all along the 'shore, there seemed to be millions of them.

'Why in the world are you throwing starfish into the water?' he asked the boy as he approached.

'If these starfish are on the beach tomorrow morning when the tide goes out they will die,' replied the boy, continuing with his work.

'But that's ridiculous!' cried the man. 'Look around you. There are thousands of miles of beach and millions of starfish. How can you believe that what you're doing could possibly make a difference?'

The young boy picked up another starfish, paused thoughtfully, and remarked as he tossed it out into the waves, 'It makes a difference to this one.'

MORAL

What is never attempted will never be accomplished; even the smallest of efforts defeats apathy.

REFLECTION

The tale can be used to illustrate the importance of breaking a task down into small, achievable units, and having the faith and confidence to start.

Who or what are the 'starfish' that you want to save?
What goal are you trying to achieve at the moment?
In what way might you break it down into chunks?
Is your goal worth the effort you might expend? Why?
How will you keep your resolve to start – and finish the task?

4

INTRODUCTION

This story is a good way of encouraging people to truly explore the notion of goal setting, to ensure that they are working towards not just realistic, sensible and achievable goals, but also goals that they actually want! You know the saying – if you don't have goals for yourself, you'll end up helping everybody else achieve theirs!

THE TALE

The Wise Fisherman

An American businessman on holiday in Mexico was standing on the pier of a small coastal village, when a tiny boat with just one fisherman pulled alongside. Inside the boat were some large and very healthy-looking tuna fish. The American complimented the Mexican on the quality of his fish and asked how long it had taken him to catch them.

The Mexican replied, 'Not long, Senõr, I have been out in my boat for a few hours only.'

The American, somewhat puzzled, then said, 'You are obviously a good fisherman, and these are very healthy-looking fish, so why don't you stay out longer and catch some more?'

The Mexican laughed. 'Why would I want to do that, Senõr? I make enough money to support me and my family. I do not need to catch more fish.'

The American then asked, 'But what do you do with the rest of your time?'

The Mexican fisherman said, 'I am completely free to do whatever I want. I play with my children, take siesta with my wife, stroll into the village every evening where I sip wine and play guitar with my amigos. I have a full and rewarding life, Senõr.'

The American scoffed, 'Ah, you may think so now...' He took out his business card. 'I am a Harvard graduate in business management and I can help you. The way I see it – you should spend more time fishing each day,   and with the proceeds of what you catch you can buy a bigger boat. After some time you could sell the bigger boat and buy several boats, and eventually you would have your own fleet. We'd need to hire more fishermen, of course, but don't worry. I know just the person to help us recruit them.'

By now, the American had produced a pad and pen, and was busily drawing flow charts and diagrams.

'In a few years,' he continued, 'instead of selling your catch to a middleman, you would sell directly to the processor, eventually opening your own cannery. That way, you would control the product, the processing and the distribution. Of course, you would need to leave this village and move to, say, Mexico City. We'd need to increase your profile in the market, you understand. From there, you'd probably move to Los Angeles and eventually to New York, where you could control your successful and expanding business.'

The American stopped, somewhat out of breath, and waited for the fisherman's grateful acceptance of his advice. The Mexican fisherman pondered. 'But, Senõr, how long will this all take?'

The American, now working on his Psion calculator and scribbling on his pad, replied, 'Oh, I should say somewhere in the region of 15 to 20 years.'

'But what then, Senõr?'

The American laughed and said, 'That's the really clever part. When the time is right – and I should be happy to advise you – you could float the company on the stock market, sell your stock to the public and become very rich. You would make millions.'

'Millions, Senõr?' asked the fisherman, rubbing his chin. 'And after that, what then?'

The American said, 'Well, eventually you would be able to retire a wealthy man, and choose exactly the life you wanted for you and your family. For example, you might move to a small coastal fishing village. You would be completely free to do what you want. You could play with your children, take siesta with your wife and stroll into the village each evening, where you could sip wine and play guitar with your amigos. You could have a full and rewarding life.'

The fisherman thought for a moment and then said, 'Thank you for the advice, Senõr, but if you don't mind I think I'll save myself the 15 years, and stay right where I am!'

MORAL

Be sure that the goal you think you want is actually what you do want, and that you haven't been persuaded by some well-meaning management consultant!

REFLECTION

Do your goals fit with your life's values?
What is the goal that you are trying to achieve?
Are you sure this is your goal? Why do you want to achieve this?
What will happen if you achieve this goal? What will it bring you?
What will happen if you don't achieve it?
Who influences you in your goal setting?
What are your long- and short-term goals? Do they support each other?

5

INTRODUCTION

Nobody is too sure as to who originally 'invented' the Mullah Nasrudin, but he is a fictional character who surfaces in numerous generations and on different continents. He is the epitome of the idiot savant or jester character, whose simplistic words of wisdom can carry meaning at many different levels of learning. The Sufis (marvellous coaches!) traditionally used teaching tales such as these for therapeutic exercise. Their students would be asked to choose tales that they particularly related to, and to meditate on them, and it was thought that in this way they would access a higher wisdom, the kind of wisdom that comes only from within. This one is a favourite of mine – don't be fooled by its brevity. The discussions that arise from it can go on for hours!

THE TALE

Let There be Light

Late one night a man was walking home when he came across the Mullah Nasrudin on his hands and knees underneath a street light, apparently searching for something on the ground.

'What are you looking for, Mullah?' the man asked as he approached.

'I'm searching for the key to my house,' replied Nasrudin, still on his hands and knees.

'Let me help you,' replied the man, and he quickly got down on all fours next to Nasrudin and started scouring the dirt next to him, underneath the street light.

After a few unproductive minutes, the man asked, 'Nasrudin, where exactly did you drop your key?'

The Mullah pointed behind him into the dark street, 'Over there, in my own house.'

'Then why on earth are you looking for it here?' asked his companion, incredulously.

'Because there is more light here than in my own house,' replied the Mullah.

MORAL

Always be sure that you are searching for the right thing in the right place!

REFLECTION

You can use this tale to discuss issues such as goal setting, envisioning the future, achieving goals and problem solving.

What is your goal, or what are you searching for?
Are you searching for this goal in the right place?
Are you looking for a key? What does this key open?
What represents the 'darkness' and 'light' in your life or in your work?
Who else can help you look for the key?
How long will you carry on looking?
What will happen when you find the key? What will happen if you don't find it?

6

INTRODUCTION

I am grateful to my friends Jan Stewart and Dick McCann for letting me tell this story. It's a very good tale to tell to entrepreneurs, autocratic leaders or those working in a power culture. I think it illustrates well the problems inherent in empire building!

THE TALE

The Spider

The spider found a perfect place for her home. It was under the eaves of an old house and sheltered well from the weather, but not the passing insects.

She began to spin her web and worked quickly to complete the task, her mind constantly fantasizing about the delicious meals she could expect to catch. At first her web was small, as she concentrated on strong foundations. Then she constructed the radial arms and began to weave an enormous expanse of intricately spun silk. The web shimmered in the sunlight as it spread out in all directions.

By early evening, the web was finished. As the insects emerged to enjoy the dusk, she was awaiting her first victims, smug in her superior lair. Hundreds of midges and winged ants flew by that evening and many of them were captured by the web. She paralysed them with her venom and moved them to her storehouse at one end of the web. This was her best haul for a long time. She had more food tonight than she could eat in a week.

However, this spider was greedy! In her selfish desire to look after her own needs she had ignored the other spiders who had been living under the eaves long before her. Her web was purposely spun over the top of their webs so as to intercept most of the insects. Only a few penetrated her threads to be caught in the other webs. At first the other spiders tried to damage her web but she would mend it quickly and damage their webs in return. She was fearful that someone would take over her position in the eaves and guarded her territory zealously.

Each time her web needed repairing, she would strengthen the edges and extend them a little further, slowly encroaching upon the territory of the other spiders. They soon gave up and moved on, leaving her to reign supreme.

Her enormous web was hard to maintain. Each night 20 to 30 insects were caught and these placed an immense strain on the fibres. They began to sag and eventually broke in several places. The dry summer weather was also affecting her web as the dust hung heavily on the sticky silk threads.

Eventually, the web broke and became impossible to repair. She would have to abandon it and start all over again in a new location.

(From *Aesop's Management Fables* by McCann and Stewart, Butterworth-Heinemann. Reprinted by permission of Butterworth-Heinemann Publishers, a division of Reed Educational & Professional Publishing Ltd.)

MORAL

Be careful what you set your sights on; you might be a victim of your own success.

REFLECTION

Use this story to discuss such issues as personal and team goal setting, achievement, styles of leadership and working with others.

How can you relate this story to your own or other's organizations?
In what way are you, or someone you know, like the spider?
Have you thought through your goals and what you want to achieve?
Are you setting your goals too high?
If you achieve your goals, how will you maintain them?
How could you work more collaboratively with others?

7

INTRODUCTION

This retold story has appeared in various guises over the years. I have used it to help people who are working on finding their own goals and sense of direction. It works well in encouraging them to take a flexible approach to achieving the goal and also to question how other people achieve theirs!

THE TALE

Arrows

There was once a warrior who in his time had been a mighty adversary and a master in all forms of war – except archery. Tiring of his career, he decided to retire and spend the rest of his days studying the art of archery. He discovered a monastery where they taught the skill, and he happily studied there for 10 years. At the end of this time, the abbot came to him and said, 'My son, we have taught you all there is to know about archery. It is time for you to leave us.'

With a heavy heart, the warrior left the monastery and for some time wandered alone until he came to what had been his old village. To his amazement, as he entered the village he noticed a bull's eye on a tree, with an arrow sticking out right from the centre.

'Whoever shot that arrow must be a fine marksman,' said the warrior to himself.

He hadn't gone much further when he saw another bull's eye, and another and another – and all of them had arrows in the centre of the target.

The warrior decided he must know who this amazing master archer was, as there was surely much that he could learn from him. He enquired of the elders of the town, and said, 'Whoever that marksman is, ask him to meet me today, in one hour's time. I'll be waiting by the river at the edge of the village.'

Sure enough, one hour later, the warrior stood waiting by the river. But there was no one there – except a little girl playing on the bank. She noticed him and came over to where he was standing.

'Are you waiting for someone, sir?' she enquired, looking up at him. The warrior shooed her away.

'Run along, little girl, be on your way.'

'But,' the little girl continued, 'I think I might be able to help. You see, you look to me like you're waiting for someone, and I was told to meet someone here this afternoon, too.'

The warrior looked at her incredulously.

'It is true,' he said, 'I am waiting for someone. I am waiting to meet the finest archer in the land, the one who is responsible for shooting all these perfect shots I see all over this village.'

'Then this is a happy meeting,' said the girl. 'For I am the person who made all those shots.'

More suspicious than ever, the man bent down and looked at her.

'If you're telling me the truth,' he said, 'tell me how exactly you got a perfect shot every time with your arrow.'

'That's easy,' replied the girl. 'I just point my bow very straight, and let the arrow fly. Then wherever it lands, I draw a bull's eye.'

MORAL

Not everything is as it seems!

REFLECTION

You can use this tale to address such issues as goal setting, practical ways to achieve goals, and seeing problems or issues in a different way.

How are you, or someone you know, like the warrior in the story?
What represents the 'bull's eye' in your life or in your work?
Are you taking a rigid view of shooting the arrow?
Are you making achieving your target harder than it needs to be?
What would be a different way of viewing the target and arrow?
How might you change the target?

8

INTRODUCTION

I, like thousands of other children, grew up with Winnie-the-Pooh. A family ritual that developed in my early childhood (and I'm blessed if I can remember how or why!) was that my Auntie Kate and I used to read Pooh to each other every Saturday. I think if the truth be known, I used to read and she used to have a quiet forty winks! Even though he is a self-confessed 'Bear of Very Little Brain', Winnie-the-Pooh still has a lot to offer us in his simple philosophies of life.

THE TALE

In Which Pooh and Piglet Go Hunting

One fine winter's day, when Piglet was brushing away the snow in front of his house, he happened to look up and there was Winnie-the-Pooh. Pooh was walking round and round in a circle, thinking of something else, and when Piglet called to him, he just went on walking.

'Hallo!' said Piglet. 'What are you doing?'

'Hunting,' said Pooh.

'Hunting what?'

'Tracking something,' said Winnie-the-Pooh very mysteriously.

'Tracking what?' said Piglet, coming closer.

'That's just what I ask myself. I ask myself, What?'

'What do you think you'll answer?'

'I shall have to wait until I catch up with it,' said Winnie-the-Pooh. 'Now look there.' He pointed to the ground in front of him. 'What do you see there?'

'Tracks,' said Piglet. 'Paw-marks.' He gave a little squeak of excitement. 'Oh, Pooh! Do you think it's a – a – a – Woozle?'

'It may be,' said Pooh. 'Sometimes it is, and sometimes it isn't. You never can tell with paw-marks.'

With these few words he went on tracking, and Piglet, after watching him for a minute or two, ran after him. Winnie-the-Pooh had come to a sudden stop, and was bending over the tracks in a puzzled sort of way.

'What's the matter?' asked Piglet.

'It's a very funny thing,' said Bear, 'but there seem to be two animals now. This – whatever-it-was – has now been joined by another – whatever-it-is – and the two of them are now proceeding in company. Would you mind coming with me, Piglet, in case they turn out to be Hostile Animals?'

Piglet scratched his ear in a nice sort of way, and said that he had nothing to do until Friday, and would be delighted to come, in case it really was a Woozle.

'You mean, in case it really is two Woozles,' said Winnie-the-Pooh, and Piglet said that anyhow he had nothing to do until Friday. So off they went together.

There was a small spinney of larch trees just here, and it seemed as if the two Woozles, if that is what they were, had been going round this spinney; so round this spinney went Pooh and Piglet after them...

Suddenly Winnie-the-Pooh stopped, and pointed excitedly in front of him. 'Look!'

'*What?*' said Piglet, with a jump. And then, to show that he hadn't been frightened, he jumped up and down once or twice more in an exercising sort of way.

'The tracks!' said Pooh. '*A third animal has joined the other two!*'

'Pooh!' cried Piglet. 'Do you think it is another Woozle?'

'No,' said Pooh, 'because it makes different marks. It is, either Two Woozles and one, as it might be, Wizzle, or Two, as it might be, Wizzles and one, if so it is, Woozle. Let us continue to follow them.'

So they went on, feeling just a little anxious now, in case the three animals in front of them were of Hostile Intent. And then, all of a sudden, Winnie-the-Pooh stopped again, and licked the tip of his nose, in a cooling manner, for he was feeling more hot and anxious than ever in his life before. *There were four animals in front of them!*

'Do you see, Piglet? Look at their tracks! Three, as it were, Woozles, and one, as it was, Wizzle. *Another Woozle has joined them!*'

And so it seemed to be. There were the tracks; crossing over each other here, getting muddled up with each other there; but, quite plainly every now and then, the tracks of four sets of paws.

'I think,' said Piglet, when he had licked the tip of his nose too, and found that it brought very little comfort, 'I think that I have just remembered something. I have just remembered something that I forgot to do yesterday and shan't be able to do tomorrow. So I suppose I really ought to go back and do it now.'

'We'll do it this afternoon, and I'll come with you,' said Pooh.

'It isn't the sort of thing you can do in the afternoon,' said Piglet quickly. 'It's a very particular morning thing, that has to be done in the morning, and, if possible, between the hours of – what would you say the time was?'

'About 12,' said Winnie-the-Pooh, looking at the sun.

'Between, as I was saying, the hours of 12 o'clock and five past 12. So really, dear old Pooh, if you'll excuse me – *What's that?*'

Pooh looked up at the sky, and then, as he heard the whistle again, he looked up into the branches of a big oak tree, and then he saw a friend of his.

'It's Christopher Robin,' he said.

'Ah, then you'll be all right,' said Piglet. ' You'll be quite safe with *him*. Good-bye.' And he trotted off home as quickly as he could, very glad to be Out of All Danger again.

Christopher Robin came slowly down from his tree.

'Silly old Bear,' he said, 'what *were* you doing? First you went round the spinney twice by yourself, and then Piglet ran after you and you went round again together, and then you were just going round a fourth time...'

'Wait a moment,' said Winnie-the-Pooh, holding up his paw. He sat down and thought in the most thoughtful way he could think. Then he fitted his paw into one of the Tracks...and then scratched his nose twice and stood up.

'Yes,' said Winnie-the-Pooh. 'I have been Foolish and Deluded,' said he, 'and I am a Bear of No Brain at All.'

'You're the Best Bear in All the World,' said Christopher Robin.

'Am I?' said Pooh hopefully. And then he brightened up suddenly. 'Anyhow,' he said, 'it is nearly Luncheon Time.' So he went home for it.

(From *Pooh and Piglet Go Hunting and Nearly Catch a Woozle* by A A Milne, illustrated by E H Shepard, from *Winnie-the-Pooh* by A A Milne, illustrated by E H Shepard, © 1926 by E P Dutton, renewed 1954 by A A Milne. Used by permission of Dutton Children's Books, an imprint of Penguin Putnam Books for Young Readers, a division of Penguin Putnam Inc.)

MORAL

Are you going round in circles in your life?

REFLECTION

You can use this tale to discuss issues such as learning from your mistakes, learning with others and taking a global view to goal setting.

What represents the 'Woozle' or goal in your life or in your work?
What represents the 'spinney of trees' in your life or in your work?
How long have you been hunting and how long will you carry on?
Christopher Robin saw the situation clearly from the tree above. What could help you to see the situation more clearly?

9

INTRODUCTION

I've never been a golfer myself, but Steve Warren, who is a life coach, is an avid one, so much so that he writes and sells books and audiotapes on the subject, telling other would-be golfers how to improve their game. This is a story he uses with his coachees to illustrate what happens when you start thinking about your goal in a negative way.

THE TALE

Golf Story

Some years ago I was due to take part in a knock-out final; it was against a chap whose handicap was better than mine, so I was quite nervous about playing against him. However, as soon as I found out that I was going to be in the final I started my mental preparation. Some three weeks before the game, I set myself a goal – and that was to win! I wrote down my goal every day and visualized myself winning. I also resolved to believe in myself and told myself over and over that I would win. By the time it came to the day of the contest I felt confident and raring to go.

It was going to be a long day – the final was over 36 holes – and I knew that I would have to stay focused if I was to win. However, I didn't get off to a very good start and, after the first two holes, my opponent was ahead and I started to feel myself sinking into negative self-talk, beating myself up for beginning poorly. But I took some deep breaths and said to myself, 'Come on, Steve, there's a long way to go. You've played well to get to the final, and there's no reason why you shouldn't win.'

It was critical for me to let go of those negative thoughts and forget about the shots I'd just played. They were history – there was no point in analysing what was in the past. I had to focus on the present, concentrating my mind on playing just one shot at a time. With a more confident attitude, I then went on to win the next two holes, which brought me back on level terms.

For the next few holes we stayed evenly matched, and then, as we walked to the next part of the course, my opponent suddenly turned to me and said, 'I don't mind losing so long as it's not by a big margin like seven and six.' (For those of you that don't play golf, losing seven and six means you are seven holes behind with six holes to play – game over!) Well, I don't know if he saw my jaw drop to the floor! Why was he talking like this? We were still only a quarter of the way round the course, we had 27 holes left to play and the game could quite easily have gone either way. This was music to my ears. In my opponent's mind he had already lost – and he was more concerned about the supposed embarrassment of losing by a big margin than actually losing!

As we continued the game, I kept talking positively to myself, and staying focused on each shot. However, I noticed that his negative self-talk became more noticeable; he started to curse his luck, the weather and the bounce of the ball, and spent less time concentrating on trying to win the game. Consequently, he started to play poorly.

Our match finished on the 30th hole and the winning score was seven and six – exactly the score that my opponent had dreaded losing by. Although I was obviously delighted that I had won, I was also genuinely sorry to see my opponent talk himself into defeat.

(From *Think Your Way to Better Golf* by Steve Warren.
Reproduced with permission.)

MORAL

Be careful to focus on success rather than failure.

REFLECTION

Use this story to discuss such issues as positive goal setting, positive thinking and focusing on solutions rather than problems.

In what way is your life/work like a game of golf?
Are you setting yourself positive or negative goals?
Are you talking yourself into defeat?
Are you concentrating on the solution or on the problem?
Are you focusing on the present – or spending too much time reflecting on the past?

10

INTRODUCTION

This short but light-hearted tale, which features in The Aladdin Factor by Jack Canfield, is a good one to use with people who are setting goals and targets or maybe offering products or services, but who tend to set their sights too low or who have no real knowledge of what they have to offer. People tend to pitch themselves lower rather than higher.

THE TALE

The Ignorant Thief

A story is told of a thief in ancient times who stole a magnificent coat. The coat was made of the finest materials including buttons of silver and gold. When he returned to his friends after selling the coat to a merchant in the marketplace, his closest friend asked him how much he had sold the coat for.

'A hundred pieces of silver,' was his reply.

'You mean to tell me you only got 100 pieces of silver for that magnificent coat?' asked his friend.

'Is there a number higher than 100?' asked the thief.

(From *The Aladdin Factor* by Jack Canfield and Mark Victor Hansen.
© Jack Canfield and Mark Victor Hansen, 1995. Used by permission of
G P Putnam's Sons, a division of Penguin Putnam Inc.)

MORAL

Be sure you know the value of what you have to offer – and be prepared to ask for it!

REFLECTION

Use this story for discussing realistic and challenging goals and how they can be achieved successfully. It can also be used to discuss issues such as self-worth.

In what way are you, or someone you know, like the ignorant thief?
What represents the 'magnificent coat' that you have to sell?
Do you know the true value of the product or service you have to offer?
What might you compare against?
Are you undervaluing yourself in some way?

Problem Solving

'How Are You Going To Achieve It?'

Stories included in this section are to help people to appreciate their own strengths and capabilities, to give them hope to keep trying, to break down and analyse different parts of a problem and not to be afraid to apply different solutions.

11

INTRODUCTION

Myths and legends were originally told to help us to make sense of the world around us – and they continue to serve that purpose today. Gordius was probably the first advocator of creative thinking – and Alexander the Great the first one to use it! I have told this tale to encourage people to take a risk and challenge the rules.

THE TALE

The Gordian Knot

In ancient Greek mythology, Gordius, who was King of Phrygia and Midas's father, had declared that whoever could untie the 'Gordian knot' was destined to become ruler of all Asia. Many had tried to solve the puzzle and untie the knot but none had succeeded.

When Alexander the Great came to Phrygia he too tried his hand at the task but with as little success as everyone else. Eventually, growing impatient, he drew out his sword and smashed it down on the knot, cutting it clean in half. Even though he had not untied the knot in the way that Gordius had expected, it nevertheless had to be said that he had solved the puzzle and done what had been asked of him. Alexander was awarded the prize and he became ruler of all Asia.

MORAL

There is more than one way to untie a knot.

REFLECTION

You can use this story to illustrate the need for creative and lateral thinking, and the need to sometimes challenge 'the rules'.

What problem represents the 'knot' that you are trying to untie?
Who has invented the rules? What rules might you need to challenge?
What different approaches might you use in order to solve the problem?
How might you 'reframe' the problem?
What do you stand to win when you have untied the knot?

12

INTRODUCTION

Now, I'm not a technophobe – in fact it's hard now to imagine life without computers, mobile phones and the Internet. But I am often concerned at the degree of trust and faith that some people seem to have in the technology that they use, compared with the apparent lack of trust and faith that they show in themselves and their own abilities. This is a simple, 'low-tech' tale to illustrate the point.

THE TALE

Tiger Teaching

Mama Tiger and Baby Tiger were out hunting in the jungle. They had had a very productive day, and were now lying down underneath a tree, sleeping off their meal and relaxing in the warm afternoon sun.

All of a sudden, in the distance, Baby Tiger saw a hunter coming towards them.

'Mama, Mama, wake up!' he shouted. 'There is a hunter out to get us!'

'Hush, child,' said the Mama Tiger.

'But, Mama,' squeaked the youngster, 'he has at least three rifles, some special computerized sighting scopes and other hi-tech devices to let him see in the dark. We're doomed!'

'Watch,' said the Mama Tiger, 'and learn.'

While the hunter's back was turned, the Mama Tiger taught her cub how to slowly and silently sneak up from behind – and pounce!

Sadly, the hunter never lived to tell the tale, but Baby Tiger always remembered the lesson.

MORAL

Technology is all very well in its place – but you can't beat a good basic education.

REFLECTION

Use this story to discuss such issues as problem solving, learning, coaching and mentoring, and using experience.

What skills do you need to learn in order to do your job?
How do you presently learn these skills? What is your preferred learning style?
How can technology help you? Where can it not help you?
Who is the 'Mama Tiger' in your company or organization that you could learn from?
Who outside your company or organization could you learn from?
Whose knowledge, skills and teaching ability might you emulate?

13

INTRODUCTION

Kahlil Gibran has become well-known throughout the world as a poet, philosopher and artist. It is strange to realize that The Prophet *was written in the 1920s as the words still seem so fresh today. I think this poem is particularly relevant for coaches and their coachees. Although the subject is 'talking', he advocates more the power of silence and thinking than talking for the sake of it.*

THE TALE

The Prophet – on Talking

And then a scholar said, Speak of Talking,
And he answered, saying:
You talk when you cease to be at peace with your thoughts;
And when you can no longer dwell in the solitude of your heart you live in your lips, and sound is a diversion and a pastime.
And in much of your talking, thinking is half murdered.
For thought is a bird of space, that in a cage of words may indeed unfold its wings but cannot fly.
There are those among you who seek the talkative through fear of being alone.
The silence of aloneness reveals to their eyes their naked selves and they would escape.
And there are those who talk, and without knowledge or forethought reveal a truth which they themselves do not understand.
And there are those who have the truth within them, but they tell it not in words.
In the bosom of such as these the spirit dwells in rhythmic silence.
When you meet your friend on the roadside or in the marketplace, let the spirit in you move your lips and direct your tongue.
Let the voice within your voice speak to the ear of his ear;
For his soul will keep the truth of your heart as the taste of the wine is remembered.
When the colour is forgotten and the vessel is no more.

(From *The Prophet* by Kahlil Gibran, 1926, Penguin.)

MORAL

It is wiser to think before you speak.

REFLECTION

You can use this poem to discuss the need for thinking and silence as well as talking in any communication situation, but particularly in the context of coaching.

As a coach, do you listen more than you talk?
Are you, or others you know, frightened of silences?
Are you 'at peace with your thoughts' as Gibran suggests?
Do you, or others you know, talk through fear of being alone?
How can you ensure that your talking comes 'from the heart'?

14

INTRODUCTION

Many people have heard of the inventor Thomas Edison and most people have heard of light bulbs! I find the detail of this story, in true oral tradition, can vary somewhat in the number of times poor old Edison was supposed to have struggled with his light bulb formula. But, also in true storytelling fashion, the more the 'truth' gets embroidered, the more we tend to remember it. And I'm sure Edison wouldn't have minded being misquoted in the interests of people 'seeing the light'.

THE TALE

Edison and the Light Bulb

Thomas Edison, the American inventor, is thought of as being one of the most creative and intelligent men in history – and yet, the history books tell us that he attended his school in Michigan for only three months before being expelled at the age of 12 because his teachers thought he was educationally subnormal. In later years, Edison was to become famous for his saying 'genius is 1 per cent inspiration and 99 per cent perspiration'.

This was certainly true for him in his attempts to convert electricity into light, one of his most famous endeavours. He was reputed to have tried and failed *over 1,000 times* to perfect the incandescent electric light bulb, and when advised by his colleagues and friends to give up the whole project because it was doomed to failure, replied with total conviction and some surprise: 'Why, I haven't failed; I've just found a thousand ways in which my formula doesn't work!'

It was as much Edison's positive and tenacious attitude to endeavour and problem solving as his obvious intelligence and creativity that, in the end, were his most powerful allies.

MORAL

There is no failure – only feedback!

REFLECTION

You can use this story to illustrate the need for creative and lateral thinking, and the need to view 'failure' as a natural part of the creative process. Beware of the dangers of 'self-fulfilling prophecy'.

What represents the 'light bulb' that you are currently trying to invent?
What different approaches have you used in order to solve the problem?
What will be your motivation for continuing with this project?
How did you perceive any failures that you have had in trying to solve the problem?
How might you 'reframe' these failures like Edison did?
What projects have you given up because you thought you had failed? Could they be rekindled?

15

INTRODUCTION

I sometimes hear coaches say to their coachees such phrases as 'Oh, it's easy! A child could do it' and I think that this can be quite dangerous language to use. By whose standards is it 'easy' – yours or mine? What happens if I don't find it as easy as you tell me it's going to be? This is a true, sad and cautionary tale to illustrate the point.

THE TALE

It's Easy!

Some years ago, when my job started to entail major travelling around this country and beyond, and spending long, lonely days and nights in hotels and other dubious venues, I decided that I could either become an alcoholic – or take up knitting again.

Now, I c*an* knit, and have in the past come up with some pretty reasonable offerings – almost wearable in some cases. But I had got out of the habit of doing it, and lost what little confidence I used to have in my abilities. So I took myself off to a local knitting and sewing shop in order to reacquaint myself with the ancient art.

Looking around the shop I noticed a bright and stunning creation, a long-sleeved sweater hanging proudly on one of the walls. It was covered in cables and crossovers and other frightening patterns and I couldn't even begin to work out the mechanics. Its presence was obviously supposed to be an incentive from the shop people to all would-be knitters: 'look what you might achieve with our help.'

I was approached by one of the sales assistants. 'Can I help you?'

She was a mature, self-assured looking woman of around 50, I should say, who had one of those rather simpering, self-satisfied smiles that says 'I can do something you can't do.'

'It's been a long time since I've done any knitting...' I began, sounding rather like someone going into a confessional box for absolution, 'so, do you think I could knit *that*?'

Together we gazed – me with awe and wonderment, her with obvious pride and a touch of superiority I thought – at the stunning example on the wall.

'Of course,' she replied, smugly. '*It's easy!*'

Filled with confidence by her remark, I made the decision, and bought the minimum but, according to my new found adviser, absolutely necessary requirements – wool, needles, cable hooks, row counters, threads, pins, pattern, string and bottle of tranquillizers – that were needed to make the sweater. It probably cost me three times the ready-made equivalent, but I didn't consider this. *I was now a woman on a mission.*

I couldn't wait to get all the accoutrements home and get started. And in fact, for the first few inches, it all went rather swimmingly. But then, as all the experienced knitters amongst you will know, we reached 'the pattern'.

Well, if I tell you that all hell broke loose, it wouldn't be an exaggeration. There were needles, stitches and wool here, there and everywhere, round the back, up the front and going back the way you came. Just looking at the details of the pattern on the page made your eyes go dizzy.

K1 P1 K2tog. Sl (3) p.s.s.o. C6B
K1 P1 K2tog. Sl (3) p.s.s.o. C6B
K1 P1 K2tog. Sl (3) p.s.s.o. C6B

It informed me of this endlessly and not particularly helpfully. Rather than proving to be the stress-buster that I had imagined, it became an all-consuming stress inducer. I needed total and uninterrupted concentration just to complete one row. My assistant would be calling me to the phone.

'The Chairman of IBM wants to talk to you about a million dollar contract' (slight exaggeration).

To which I would reply, 'Well, tell him he'll have to wait until I've finished this part of the pattern. Otherwise, I'll forget if I've 'pssoed' or not.'

This tortuous procedure went on for months, until I came to the conclusion that my new found hobby was doing me no good at all and decided it was time to give it up and search for a quieter pastime, one that was less damaging to my health and wellbeing.

And the sweater? Well, I did eventually finish it (it had become a matter of principle) but by the time I did it was about three years out of date. I gave up knitting shortly after that – on the grounds that it was far too dangerous and costly to boot.

I am due to start my first meeting of Alcoholics Anonymous next week.

MORAL

Is it really 'easy' or is that just your experience?

REFLECTION

You can use this anecdote to explore such issues as how different people perceive and deal with different problems, constructive problem solving, learning and feedback, and coaching others in a positive way.

What represents 'the knitting' in your life or in your work?
Has anyone told you that something was 'easy' when you thought it wasn't?
How did you feel to be told this?
Are you guilty of telling anyone you were coaching that a particular task was easy? What effect did that have?
How could you see things more from the learner's point of view?
What other words of encouragement could you use?

16

INTRODUCTION

A surprising number of common phrases and sayings originate from the Greek myths and legends. Their original purpose was to explain some of the mysteries of life, birth and death, and to provide us with guidelines on living a good and noble life. Pandora's box is probably one of the most famous, and Thomas Bulfinch is a well-known teller of the tales.

THE TALE

Pandora's Box

The first woman was named Pandora. She was made in Heaven by Jupiter with every god contributing something to perfect her. Venus gave her beauty, Mercury persuasion, Apollo music. Thus equipped, she was conveyed to Earth and presented to Epimetheus, for his wife, who gladly accepted her, though cautioned by his brother to beware of Jupiter and his gifts. Epimetheus had in his house a box in which were kept certain noxious articles. Pandora was seized with an eager curiosity to know what this box contained and one day she slipped off the lid and looked in. Forthwith there escaped a multitude of plagues for hapless man such as gout, rheumatism and colic for his body, and envy, spite and revenge for his mind, and they scattered themselves far and wide. Pandora hastened to replace the lid, but alas! The whole contents of the box had escaped, except one thing that lay at the bottom – and that was Hope.

So we see at this day, whatever evils are abroad, Hope never entirely leaves us; and while we have that, no amount of other ills can make us completely wretched.

(From *Myths of Greece and Rome* by Thomas Bulfinch, 1979, Penguin.)

MORAL

Think twice before you open the box!

REFLECTION

You can use this story to encourage people not to give up when dealing with what might seem overwhelming problems, and to remind them of the presence of Hope in all our endeavours.

What represents the 'box' that you, or someone you know, has opened?
What 'multitude of plagues' are inside?
How might you close the box again? Or is it better not to open it at all?
In what situations is it better not to be curious?
What constitutes 'Hope' for you?
How does it feel to have Hope when dealing with the content of the box?

17

INTRODUCTION

This retold tale was passed on to me by one of my clients a long time ago, so unfortunately I don't know its origins. But it's a powerful story and one that I thought was worth including in this selection. It also works well in conjunction with the tale of 'Pandora's Box'.

THE TALE

The Devil's Toolbox

Many years ago, the Devil decided to hold a sale of all the tools of his trade. He arranged them all spick and span in a glass case for all passers-by to see. And it was quite an array! There was the gleaming dagger of Jealousy, and sitting next to that was the heavy sledgehammer of Anger. In another section he laid out the bows of Greed and Want and beside them the poisoned tipped arrows of Lust and Envy. Close-by were the weapons of Fear, Pride and Hatred. Each one had been carefully presented, and labelled with its name and corresponding price.

But in a section all on its own, quite separate from the rest, was a small, unimpressive, and rather battered looking wedge of wood, which the Devil had labelled '*Discouragement*'. Surprisingly, the price of this tool was higher than all the others put together.

When asked the reason for the difference, the Devil replied, 'The reason I value this tool so highly is that it is the one tool in my armoury that I know I can always rely on if the others fail.' He caressed the little piece of wood lovingly.

'If I can just drive this wedge into a person's mind,' the Devil said, 'it opens up the door for everything else.' He smiled. 'There is nothing quite so deadly as Discouragement.'

MORAL

Beware of the destructive power of Discouragement.

REFLECTION

You can use this tale to give people encouragement when dealing with and managing problems and issues, and to beware of the dangers of the 'D' word!

What represents 'the Devil's tools' in your life or in your work?
Have you, or someone you know, allowed discouragement to sneak into your life? What effect did this have?
How might you prevent discouragement from taking hold?
Who or what might give you encouragement?

18

INTRODUCTION

When I am witness to any organization going through a process of change (including my own I might add!), I am particularly reminded of this section out of Alice in Wonderland. Everything seems to be happening at once, no one seems to have established any rules, and nobody seems terribly sure as to who the winner is. As Alice remarks 'a very difficult game indeed'.

THE TALE

Alice and the Croquet Ground

Alice thought she had never seen such a curious croquet ground in all her life; it was all ridges and furrows; the balls were live hedgehogs; the mallets live flamingos, and the soldiers had to double themselves up and to stand on their hands and feet to make the arches.

The chief difficulty Alice found at first was in managing her flamingo: she succeeded in getting its body tucked away, comfortably enough, under her arm, with its legs hanging down, but generally, just as she had its neck nicely straightened out, and was going to give the hedgehog a blow with its head, it *would* twist itself round and look up in her face, with such a puzzled expression that she could not help bursting out laughing: and when she had got its head down, and was going to begin again, it was very provoking to find that the hedgehog had unrolled itself, and was in the act of crawling away: besides all this, there was generally a ridge or furrow in the way wherever she wanted to send the hedgehog to, and, as the doubled-up soldiers were always getting up and walking off to other parts of the ground, Alice soon came to the conclusion that it was a very difficult game indeed...

(From *Alice's Adventures in Wonderland* by
Lewis Carroll, 1865, Penguin.)

MORAL

Don't underestimate the variables and complexities of change.

REFLECTION

Use this story to discuss such issues as managing change and dealing with the problems that can arise during a period of change.

What changes are you, or someone you know, going through at the moment?
What are the variables involved in the change? How can you manage all the variables?
What direction are you aiming for?
What 'game' could you most relate to in this situation – croquet, tennis, golf?
What are the rules of the game?
How will you learn how to play it?

19

INTRODUCTION

Many people, when they look at problems and how they might overcome them, focus on the enormity of the 'big picture' and engage in problem-solving on a grand scale, forgetting about some of the smaller issues that, if you ignore them, can end up becoming big issues. This true story, told to me by my bank manager (for a small fee obviously), is a good example of the perils of this process.

THE TALE

Look After the Pennies

On 31 December 1999, the world held its breath – in particular, hospital staff, air traffic controllers, computer programmers, and financial houses. Everyone knew of course, as they laughed confidently together, that the millennium bug wouldn't affect them; everyone knew that the computers would carry on working and that planes flying over the Atlantic at midnight would still be flying a minute after midnight – but still, nobody wanted to be the one 30,000 feet up in the air to find out.

Most national banks in the UK had spent thousands, and in some cases millions, of pounds during 1999 on planning, researching and consulting, in the hope that the transition into the next century would go relatively smoothly. The bank that I use in the city of York in the north of England was no exception. On 3 January, the first business day after the New Year, the bank manager of the York branch sat down at his desk, inwardly breathing a sigh of relief. No problems seemed to have occurred over the holiday period. Nothing had blown up, broken down or developed a life of its own.

Starting to relax, he sat down to open his mail for that day, which included the usual correspondence, memos to read and letters to sign. Suddenly aware that something wasn't quite right, he looked down to the bottom of a letter he had been reading, where the administration assistant had stamped the corner to confirm receipt:

RECEIVED 3 JANUARY 1900

Apparently, the million pound millennium conversion package had not included changing the rubber date stamp!

MORAL

In your concern for the big picture, don't trip up over the small problems.

REFLECTION

Use this story to discuss such issues as the size and nature of problems, planning, prioritizing and attention to detail.

What problems or issues do you, or someone you know, currently face?
What are the big issues? What are the small issues?
Which issues do you need to tackle first?
Which issues can be left until later, or delegated to someone else?
What 'small' problems might become big ones if ignored?

20

INTRODUCTION

Whatever your religious or spiritual beliefs, the Bible is still a good source of teaching stories, and the story of David and Goliath *must be one of the best known. Whether you use it in its full story format, or just as an extended metaphor, it is still an inspiring example of courage and faith overcoming adversity.*

THE TALE

David and Goliath

David's family lived in Bethlehem, just south of Jerusalem, and David was the youngest of eight sons. While his three eldest brothers were away fighting in King Saul's army, David took care of his father's sheep in the fields around Bethlehem. He was a diligent shepherd, and would do anything to keep his flock free from harm. Sometimes wild animals would try to steal the lambs, but David was strong and fearless, and would fight and kill the wild animals in order to rescue the lambs.

The people of Israel, David's country, were in battle against the Philistines. Amongst the Philistines' army were many giant men; the tallest and strongest of them was named Goliath. He was 10 feet tall, and struck fear into the hearts of all King Saul's soldiers. When the two armies faced each other, it was the custom for one soldier from each side to challenge the other in single combat. Goliath had already killed many of King Saul's best men.

David's father had instructed his son to take food and drink to his brothers every day, and to report back to him on what was happening on the war front. One day, when David arrived at King Saul's campsite, he could hear Goliath yelling across the valley to the soldiers of Israel. When he asked his brothers who it was making all the noise, they told him about Goliath. David knew that God would protect him, so he went to King Saul and volunteered to fight the giant.

King Saul laughed and said, 'You couldn't fight this man, David. You are a young man with no experience of war, and Goliath has been a trained soldier for many years.'

David replied, 'When I tended my father's sheep, and a lion or a bear came to attack one of the lambs, I went after them, and killed them. The Lord has delivered me from the wild animals and He will deliver me from the hand of this Philistine.'

King Saul admired the young man's courage, and said, 'Very well, but at least let me give you armour so that you will stand a chance of surviving.'

The King dressed David in a heavy iron coat and helmet and gave him a huge sword and shield to carry, but David was not used to wearing battle dress and felt uncomfortable in it. He thanked Saul for his offer of help, but said, 'If I am going to fight Goliath, I must do it in my own way. God who kept me safe from the lion and the bear will protect me now. I have faith in Him; I don't need anything else.'

He took off the armour and helmet, and put down the heavy shield and sword, and instead, picked up his wooden staff and slingshot, and took five smooth round pebbles from the ground, which he put carefully into his shepherd's pouch.

When the giant Goliath saw David, he laughed, saying, 'You insult me! Am I a dog that you come to me with just sticks and stones?'

David answered, 'You might come with a sword and spear to help you – but I have faith, which is a much greater weapon by far.'

David placed one of the smooth round stones in his sling, drew back his hand, and let the stone fly. The stone hit Goliath right in the centre of his forehead and he fell face down with a great crash onto the ground. David quickly ran up to where he was lying, took his sword from its sheath, and cut off his head.

Seeing what had happened to their champion, the remaining Philistine soldiers took to their heels and fled, but King Saul's men, inspired by David's courage, followed in hot pursuit, and won the battle.

MORAL

Faith can be much more powerful than swords and shields.

REFLECTION

You can use this story to discuss ways of tackling problems simply but effectively, having faith and determination and bringing problems down to size.

Who or what is the 'giant problem' that you, or someone you know, might be facing?
Are you imagining the problem to be bigger than it really is?
What is the 'armour' that is surplus to your needs?
What is represented by the five round stones that David used as his weapon?
Where might you find the 'faith' that David had?
How would this faith help you to tackle the problem fearlessly?
What do you stand to gain when you have killed the giant?

Reframing and Creativity

'Let's Look At This Another Way...'

Metaphors are a great way of 'seeing things from a different perspective' and this group of stories is intended to help people to change their mindset.

21

INTRODUCTION

American anthropologist Peg Neuhauser writes about the role of storytelling in organizations and encourages us to use humour whenever possible in our stories. 'It's the "glue",' she says, 'that binds a story together.' Having heard her tell this grandfather story, I have retold it to coachees to illustrate the need to be constantly questioning and flexible in our thinking.

THE TALE

The Grand Canyon Story

My grandfather was known for being a real character, and also being very stubborn with an unshakeable belief in himself. He also, as far as we know, had no sense of humour, so what happened in this story was no laughing matter as far as he was concerned.

The story is about a trip he made to the Grand Canyon with my grand-mother in the late 1930s. The particular day they arrived it was fogged in, as it often is there. He waited around until the next morning but the fog didn't lift. Well, my grandfather wasn't known for being a very patient person either, so, refusing to wait any longer, he told my grandmother that they were leaving, and they got on the train and went on to California.

From that day and for years afterwards, he would tell people that the Grand Canyon was an over-rated tourist trap. He'd been there and seen it and there was nothing to it. We tried showing him pictures but he just pushed them away, saying, 'No! That's part of the trap. They show you these kind of pictures, and then you get there and it doesn't look anything like that.'

You just couldn't reason with the man. So eventually we gave up and would just try and steer clear of the topic of the Grand Canyon.

Then my grandmother died and my grandfather remarried. Somehow, and I have no idea how, my step-grandmother got him to go back for another visit. This time it was a gorgeous day, the view was breathtaking and my grandfather was thrilled. He went into the gift shop, bought a post card with a picture of the Grand Canyon on it and wrote to my parents on the back: *'Dear Nancy and Paul, The Grand Canyon has changed a lot. Love Amos'.*

MORAL

Don't allow your own rigidity or stubbornness to obscure what might be a beautiful view.

REFLECTION

Use this story to explore the need for flexible and creative thinking, taking a different vantage point and reframing an issue or problem.

In what ways are you, or someone you know, like the grandfather in the story?
Are you too rigid in your thinking? In what way?
How could you see things differently?
Is there something or someone you ought to 'revisit'?
Is there something or someone you could see in a more positive light?
How could you get the 'fog' to lift?
Do you listen to others' views with an open mind?

22

INTRODUCTION

We all know Aesop's story of the 'sour grapes' – indeed we have taken the title into our daily speech. But it's still good to remind ourselves of the original meaning and context of the fable. There is still a lot that can be gleaned from its timeless message.

THE TALE

Sour Grapes

Once there was a hungry fox who was walking down a country lane in search of food. He happened to notice some beautiful ripe grapes hanging from a vine at the side of the road.

'Those grapes look delicious,' said the hungry fox to himself, 'but they're so high up. How am I ever going to reach them?'

He paced backwards and forwards, backwards and forwards, under the vine, and all the time he had his eye on the beautiful, juicy black grapes that swung tantalizingly just above his head. His mouth started to water the more he looked at them.

First of all the fox tried jumping up and grabbing the grapes with his teeth. But they were too far out of his reach. Then he tried climbing the tree to get to them, but his claws could not hang onto the branches and he fell down on the ground.

It was no use. No matter how hard he tried, the grapes were just beyond the fox's grasp. Eventually the fox wandered off, and shrugging his shoulders, said to himself, 'Those grapes weren't worth my trouble. They looked sour.'

MORAL

If you fail, you can always blame the circumstances!

REFLECTION

This story can be used to discuss such issues as achieving realistic goals, reframing your attitude to your goals and creative thinking.

In what way are you, or someone you know, like the fox in this fable?
What is represented by 'the grapes' in your life or work?
Why is it important to get these grapes?
Why are they so far away?
In what ways have you already tried to reach them? What other ways might you try?
Is there another goal you could aim for rather than the grapes?
In what way might it help you to think of this unattainable goal as 'sour'?

23

INTRODUCTION

Anyone who has heard or read the works of Stephen Covey will know him to be a prolific storyteller. I have expanded on one of his stories which illustrates the dangers that can occur through attempting to diagnose a problem before really understanding what the problem is. This is a cautionary tale for all those who use the 'this worked for me, so it will work for you' principle of coaching. If we really want to help, we need to first put ourselves in the world of the client, rather than expecting them to come into ours.

THE TALE

Making a Spectacle

A man was concerned about his eyesight, and so he went to see his friend, who was also an optician. His friend asked him to complete various tests, reading letters off a board, first with one eye and then the other, looking into the distance and so on, and at the end of the tests he concluded, 'Well, you're definitely short-sighted, I'm afraid, but don't worry, we can fix you up with some spectacles in no time. I tell you what,' he said, taking off his own spectacles, 'I don't normally do this, but because we're friends, and you're short of time, why don't you take mine? They're the best I've ever had!'

The man, somewhat taken aback, but not wanting to appear ungrateful, put on his friend's glasses and looked again at the letters in front of him.

'But this is hopeless,' he said. 'Everything's a blur!'

'Why, that's impossible!' said the optician. 'I've had those spectacles for five years and I've had great vision. Look again; try harder!'

'I *am* trying,' said his friend irritably. 'That just makes it worse. I can't see a thing.'

'Well, there must be something wrong with you,' concluded the optician huffily, '*I've* never had any trouble at all.'

His friend stood up, handed the spectacles back, and said, 'Look, no offence, but I think I'd better find another optician.' With that, he walked out of the room.

'Well!' said the optician, to his assistant, as they watched the man from the window. 'That's gratitude for you!'

MORAL

Just because your spectacles work for you don't expect that they will work for anyone else!

REFLECTION

Stephen Covey encourages us to 'seek first to understand then to be understood'. This story can be used to discuss such issues as appreciating other people's 'maps of the world', not attempting to 'fix' people with one solution, reframing your attitude to problems and creative thinking.

In what way can you relate to the people in the story?
What is represented by 'the spectacles' in your life or work?
How do you show your understanding of others' problems?
Have you, or someone you know, been guilty of 'fixing' someone?
How could you take a more flexible view?

24

INTRODUCTION

Most people have heard of Uncle Remus, allegedly an old black slave, working in the cotton plantations of the deep south of North America, who, when the day's work was done, would tell stories to the children about rabbits, foxes, wolves and turtles that behaved like humans. The Brer Rabbit *stories (in a similar style to Aesop's) began life as short fables, and then, in the late 1800s, were expanded on by a skilful storyteller called Joe Chandler Harris. This particular story is one of my favourites and is a good example of the technique and use of 'reverse psychology'.*

THE TALE

Brer Rabbit and the Tar Baby

Brer Fox and Brer Rabbit were sworn enemies. Brer Fox was sick of Brer Rabbit lording it about the place telling people how clever he was, and he was determined to teach the conceited animal a lesson he wouldn't forget.

He got hold of some black tar and turpentine and began to mix and mould the two together until it began to take the shape of a strange little doll. He put a little dress and a big straw hat on her head and she looked for all the world like a little Tar Baby girl.

Brer Fox, feeling pleased with his work, took the Tar Baby, his new creation, and put her in the middle of the road, where he knew Brer Rabbit would be passing by shortly.

Sure enough, after a short while, he saw the cheeky Rabbit come skipping along the road. When he saw the Tar Baby, he stopped and scratched his head.

'Now what in the world might this be?' he said to himself, but, being the well-brought up Rabbit he was, raised his hat and said, 'Morning, Ma'am.' Not surprisingly, the Tar Baby said nothing.

'Nice weather, don't you think?' continued Brer Rabbit, walking a bit closer. Still no reply. 'For the time of the year,' said Brer Rabbit, speaking more loudly now, and stepping closer still to the Tar Baby.

All the time Brer Fox was watching the proceedings from a nearby bush, and trying not to laugh. By this time, Brer Rabbit was beginning to lose his patience.

'What's the matter? You deaf?' he shouted in the Tar Baby's ear.

'I said, "Are you deaf?",' he repeated with his face against hers.

On getting no reply, Brer Rabbit said, 'Stuck up, that's what you are. And I think it's about time you learnt some manners. If you don't say "howdy" to me right now, why, I'm going to *bop* you on the nose.'

All the time Brer Fox was watching from his nearby bush, and by now his sides were aching from trying to suppress his laughter.

'Right, you've asked for it.' Brer Rabbit swung back his paw, and *bop!* He hit Tar Baby on the side of her head – and immediately became stuck. Try as he might, he couldn't get loose.

'If you don't let me go, I'm going to *bif* you on the other side of your head.'

On getting no reply, he said, 'Well, you've really asked for it this time.' *Bif!* He hit the Tar Baby on the other side of her head – and found that his other paw was stuck just as much as the first.

'Why you...' Brer Rabbit yelled, kicking out at the Tar Baby, only to find that, after a short time, both his legs were also stuck on the Tar Baby's body.

Unable to contain himself any longer, Brer Fox stepped out from his hiding place. 'Howdy, Brer Rabbit!' he said. 'You look kinda "stuck up" this morning!' He laughed and laughed until the tears poured down his cheeks.

'Guess I got you good and proper this time,' he continued. 'Not so clever now, are we? Well you can just 'stick around' while I go and light me a nice big fire ready for some yummy rabbit stew!'

Now, that Brer Rabbit was as crafty as could be – and much cleverer than old Brer Fox – and he pretended to be very frightened and upset. 'Well, I guess the cleverer of us won,' he said, 'and if I have to...g-g-go, I think I'd rather die stewed in a pan than be thrown into that *bramble patch on the hill*.' He jerked his head back as he was talking to indicate where the patch was.

Brer Fox stopped in his tracks. He hadn't expected this. And wanting to inflict as much pain as possible on his old adversary, he said, 'Maybe I can't be bothered with a fire. Maybe I'll just hang you instead.'

Brer Rabbit, who was as crafty as could be, pretended to sob when he heard this and said, 'Brer Fox, you can hang me just as high as you like, but please, please don't throw me into that *bramble patch on the hill*.'

'Ain't got no string for hanging,' said Brer Fox, again disappointed at his opponent's reaction. 'Guess I'll have to drown you.'

And Brer Rabbit, who was as crafty as could be, said, 'Drown me as deep as you like, just please, *please* don't throw me into the *bramble patch*.'

Well, Brer Fox wanted to hurt that rabbit just as much as he could, so in the end, thinking he was very smart, he plucked Brer Rabbit off the Tar

Baby, swung him once, twice, three times round his head and with all his might threw him into the bramble patch on the hill.

Feeling very pleased with himself, Brer Fox stood and waited for the howls of pain from the rabbit. But he was greeted with silence. Eventually, just when he thought that Brer Rabbit must be well and truly dead, he heard a voice in the distance, and looking up, saw the rabbit waving and calling to him from the other side of the hill.

'Thank you, Brer Fox,' he cried, 'for setting me free from the Tar Baby and throwing me into the bramble patch. By the way, didn't I tell you – I was born and raised in that bramble patch!'

MORAL

Beware of people who protest too much.

REFLECTION

Use this traditional tale to help people to 'reframe' a problem or issue and understand that there might be a number of different perspectives one could take.

> *In what way are you, or someone you know, dealing with a character like Brer Fox?*
> *What creative tactics might you use to deal with this character?*
> *What problems are you currently getting 'stuck on'?*
> *What represents the 'bramble patch' or a safe haven for you?*
> *How might you, or someone you know, use the concept of 'reverse psychology'?*

25

INTRODUCTION

This retold tale has been used, amongst others, by Marie Finlay and Christine Hogan from the Curtin University of Technology in Australia, who tell it to their human resource development students. I have used it with coachees to encourage a creative and practical thought process and to illustrate the danger of getting carried away with 'good ideas'.

THE TALE

Belling the Cat

Once upon a time, in a big old house in the country, lived a huge family of mice. For many years they had enjoyed a good life, and had the run of the kitchen and all the food they could eat.

Then, one day, disaster struck. The owners of the house, obviously concerned with the damage that the mice were causing, bought a cat. The cat, anxious to prove his worth, chased the mice all over the house, up in the attic, down in the cellars, and to their horror, caught and ate quite a few of 'the family'.

One of the mice called a crisis meeting to discuss how they should deal with the situation. Being very creative mice as they were, they brainstormed lots of ideas to bring about the demise of the cat, including 'poison it', 'shoot it', 'frighten it to death' and so on.

Eventually, one of the mice in the group piped up.

'Why don't we put a bell on the cat, so that anywhere it goes, we can hear it ringing, and this will give us time to run away and hide?'

His friends all thought this was an excellent idea, and were patting him on the back and congratulating him on his creativity. Amidst all the jubilation, a very small mouse in the corner, who had been quiet up until now, stood up and raised a paw.

'Could I ask a question?' he squeaked timidly.

'Of course,' answered the leader of the mice. 'Fire away.'

'Well, I'm sure it's a good idea and everything, and I don't want to sound like a killjoy, but…' he gulped, 'who will bell the cat?'

MORAL

Creative ideas are great – so long as someone has thought them through!

REFLECTION

This story can be used to discuss such issues as setting and achieving realistic goals, creative and realistic thinking and practical problem solving.

In what way are you, or someone you know, like the mice in the tale?
What is represented by 'the cat' that you need to deal with?
In what ways do you encourage creative ideas?
Are these ideas realistic and practical? Who ensures that they are realistic?
What are the inherent dangers of your creative idea?
Is there another (safer) way of dealing with 'the cat'?

26

INTRODUCTION

I am indebted to my friend Treeza Whitehead, another storyteller, for introducing me to this anecdote by Scott Simmerman of the Performance Management Company in the United States. Although it's one of the shortest, told in the right context, it can promote the longest discussion.

THE TALE

Two Caterpillars

Two caterpillars were sitting on a cabbage leaf having a chat. Suddenly, they heard a loud swishing noise, and looking up, saw a beautiful butterfly flying overhead. The first caterpillar looked to the other, shook his head and said, 'You'll never get me up in one of those things.'

MORAL

At some point you have to stop being a caterpillar in order to become a butterfly!

REFLECTION

This is a good story to use in the context of change management and to look at change positively *and* creatively and from different angles.

In what way are you, or someone you know, like the caterpillar?
What represents the butterfly or change for you?
Are you aware of the imminent change or are you ignorant like the caterpillar?
What will need to happen for the caterpillar to become a butterfly?
What fears might you need to address to undergo the metamorphosis?
How will your life be different?

27

INTRODUCTION

I think this is a wonderful anecdote to illustrate the need for flexibility and acceptance of change. There are several versions of the story and the original, I believe, is attributed to a writer named Frank Koch, a naval officer.

THE TALE

Changing Course

A battleship had been at sea on manoeuvres in heavy weather for several days. The captain, who was concerned about the deteriorating conditions, stayed on the bridge so that he could keep an eye on all activities. One night, shortly after dark, the lookout on the bridge suddenly shouted, 'A light, captain, bearing on the starboard bow.'

'Is it steady or moving astern?' the captain asked.

The lookout confirmed that it was steady, which meant that the battleship was apparently on a dangerous collision course with the other ship.

The captain then called to the signalman, 'Signal that ship: "We are on a collision course. Advise you change course 20 degrees north." '

Back came the response from the other ship: 'You change course 20 degrees south.'

Annoyed at the arrogance of the response, the captain said, 'Send: "I am a captain, change course 20 degrees north." '

'I am a seaman second class,' came the reply, 'you had still better change course 20 degrees south.'

By this time, the captain was furious. He shouted, 'Send: "I am a battleship. Change course 20 degrees north." '

Back came the flashing light: 'I am a lighthouse.'

The captain changed course.

MORAL

Flexibility is the key to common sense and success.

REFLECTION

Use this story to discuss such issues as changing paradigms, seeing other people's points of view and the need for flexibility.

What represents the lighthouse and the battleship for you in your life or at work?
What cannot be moved? What could be moved?
How could you see a certain situation from a different perspective?
Do you need to be more flexible? If so, how?
In what situations are you, or someone you know, steering blindly?
What represents the 'fog' for you? How could you lift this fog?

28

INTRODUCTION

If I'm ever driving round a large city that is unknown to me, and find myself getting into a bit of a panic, I say to myself, 'Now just pretend you're driving with your Mother in the passenger seat.' My mother, God bless her, had something of a nervous disposition, particularly when driving with me (can't imagine why) and it's amazing how just the thought of her sitting next to me shaking and hanging onto her safety belt, immediately shifts me into a feeling of being 'in charge'. This is a similar tale of changing perspectives.

THE TALE

Cable Cars

If you ask anyone in San Francisco if they have been on a cable car, they nod, smile enigmatically and say 'just once'.

After I'd been to the city a couple of times, I discovered why. Cable cars are probably one of the most potentially dangerous and certainly uncomfortable forms of transport that I have ever experienced. And like so many other things – big dipper wheels at the theme park, hang gliding and white water rafting (although why anybody would want to do any of these things is beyond me) – they are also very exciting.

For those who have not yet enjoyed this experience, let me try to paint the picture for you. The cars are hauled around this notoriously hilly city by very thick metal cables (hence the name!) laid very securely into the road, which your intellect tells you can't possibly snap, but your emotions don't have quite the same confidence.

The insides consist of two long parallel wooden seats facing each other, a driver at the front, and a conductor who squeezes his or her way through the crowds to check tickets, which is something else I didn't mention: these things are so popular that people literally hang off the sides.

I remember vividly the first time I rode on one; I made the mistake of wearing a rather expensive cream silk trouser suit (sounds hideous, but trust me, it was quite nice). It was early evening and some friends and I were going out for dinner. For once the cable car was quite empty. Every time the thing turned a corner, or went up a sharp hill (very common in San Francisco) I slid rather spectacularly from one end of the bench to the other. This was a marvellous ploy for cleaning the seat but not particularly good for the silk suit.

Anyway, this particular incident happened one day when I had finished my work and was going down to the popular Pier 47 with all the other tourists. The car was packed.

A family group got on – mother, father and a boy and girl of around 12 to 14. The boy appeared to be a typical teenager, spending most of the time annoying his mother, and hanging out of the windows to take photos of the views. Cable cars have a yellow line just inside the entrance, which you cross over at your peril. The driver kept telling the boy to step inside the line, but he wouldn't listen to him. It seemed the boy was impervious to any advice or request made of him.

At the next stop, two very young children, not more than eight or nine, got on the car, apparently unaccompanied. They stood on the yellow line where the rebellious teenager had been only a few minutes before. They were in serious danger of falling off as the thing hurled itself round the bends. To my amazement, the erstwhile militant stepped forward and put his arm protectively round the shoulders of the two small boys.

'Step back inside,' he told them gently, 'and then you'll be safe.'

He herded them back inside the cable car and they trustingly followed him.

I don't think his long-suffering mother noticed this unexpected act of kindness and wisdom but I wish she had. She would have seen her son in a new light.

MORAL

Give some people responsibility and they become completely different.

REFLECTION

This story illustrates how some people can apparently take on completely different characteristics, depending on circumstances and context.

How does this story relate to you or someone you know?
In what context might you see yourself differently?
Is your behaviour the same with your boss, colleagues, friends and family – or is it different?
How would you react to being given more responsibility?
Could someone you know handle more responsibility? How might it change them?

29

INTRODUCTION

In our present day culture of computer graphics, artificial intelligence and virtual reality it is sometimes difficult to tell what is reality and what isn't. I hope that this true story, which I have used many times with coachees, makes the point.

THE TALE

Trip to Vesuvius

During a holiday to southern Italy some years ago, I was persuaded to go on a day excursion to Vesuvius, the huge volcano that lies just outside the city of Naples. As part of the trip, you could experience the dubious pleasure of being taken right up to the top of the volcano, and, if you felt so inclined, actually walk inside the lip of the crater itself.

Famous for its total destruction of the town of Pompeii in the year AD 79, this volcano is still active, although it hasn't erupted since 1944, and, according to the comforting patter of the jolly guide who transports you, is now overdue by some 20 years – 'But don't let that worry you.'

It was a merry band of tourists who made the trip that morning. Not being a great lover of heights myself I was unsure as to what I was letting myself in for, but I was persuaded by the guide that the spectacular views at the top would be well worth it.

After a hair-raising coach ride, which took us the first part of the journey, we climbed (and panted) the rest of the way up to the summit. It was a long haul but I had to admit the guide was right. The view was spectacular, and all of us stood in awe, as we looked across the rim of the giant crater, watching the columns of sulphurous smoke rising slowly from the ashes. As we continued to look, silently, I was aware of two mature, and rather large women who had been in our party, puffing and panting their way to the top behind us.

'We've made it!' I heard one of them cry jubilantly.

'Great!' shouted the other. 'I can't wait.'

Excitedly they ran up to where we were standing, and I expected that they would stop and join the rest of the spectators. But to my surprise, they ran straight past us, totally ignoring the view, and rushed into the souvenir and gift shop that stood precariously on the crater's edge. Intrigued, I heard one of them shout to the other, 'I can't wait to send a postcard of this to my friends back home!'

MORAL

How often do we mistake something for 'the real thing'?

REFLECTION

You might use this story to discuss such issues as seeing a situation from different perspectives and differentiating from what is 'real' and what is 'imaginary' or superficial.

> *Things are not always as they appear. How does this story relate to you or someone you know?*
> *What 'view' might you, or someone you know, be missing?*
> *Have you been guilty of 'ignoring the view'?*
> *In what way are you focusing on the wrong picture?*
> *What does the buying of the postcard represent to you?*
> *Which problems or issues do you have that are 'real' and which 'imaginary'?*

30

INTRODUCTION

Milton Erickson was a very successful therapist operating in the United States during the 1960s and 1970s. He was known particularly for his therapeutic storytelling technique and his skill at 'reframing' a situation or problem for his patients. This tale is a nice example of using 'reverse psychology', in other words, to be seen to be condoning a patient's behaviour sometimes results in them doing the opposite.

THE TALE

Style

My daughter came home from school and said, 'Daddy, all the girls in school bite their nails and I want to be in style, too.'

I said, 'Well, you certainly ought to be in style. I think style is very important for girls. You are way behind the other girls. They have had a lot of practice. So I think the best way for you to catch up with the girls is to make sure you bite your nails enough each day. Now I think if you bite your nails for fifteen minutes three times a day, every day (I'll furnish the clock) at exactly such-and-such an hour, you can catch up.'

She began enthusiastically at first. Then she began beginning late and quitting early and one day she said, 'Daddy, I'm going to start a new style at school – long nails.'

(From *My Voice will Go with You* by Milton Erickson, 1926, ed S Rosen, WW Norton & Co Inc.)

MORAL

Making an action obligatory can take away its charm and attraction.

REFLECTION

Use this story, like Erickson, by making any 'stylish' but unwanted behaviour into an ordeal.

In what way are you, or someone you know, like the girl who bit her nails?
What is the 'stylish' but unwanted behaviour?
How might you reframe this behaviour?
Is there another, more attractive, way of 'being stylish'?

Empowerment

'You Can Do It!'

Very often people do not achieve all they want because they become disempowered. In other words, it's easier to wait for someone else to do it – and then complain! This section has stories to encourage people to realize that they always have some degree of choice in what they do.

31

INTRODUCTION

I wish I had a ham sandwich for all the times I've heard people in organizations say 'They should do this' and 'They shouldn't have done that'. It's so rare to hear anyone say, 'Do you know, I was totally responsible for that – and I messed up completely!' So, the next time you see a ham sandwich – just ponder on this story…

THE TALE

Not Ham Again!

Two men were working together on a building site. When lunchtime came, they sat down at the side of the road, and opened their respective lunchboxes. The first man, on looking into the box, rubbed his hands together gleefully and said, 'Great! I'm starved. Chicken, cheese and tuna sandwiches, crisps, a nice piece of fruit…'

The second man looked at the contents of his box and sighed heavily. 'Oh no, not ham again! I can't believe it. That's the third time this week I've had ham sandwiches. I'm getting sick and tired of seeing ham.'

'Come on, cheer up,' soothed his mate. 'Look, if you're so sick of ham sandwiches, why don't you just ask your wife to use something else?'

His mate looked puzzled. 'What are you talking about?' he said. 'I don't have a wife; I make my own sandwiches.'

MORAL

If you want a thing doing, do it yourself – but then don't complain if it goes wrong!

REFLECTION

You can use this short anecdote to discuss such issues as personal empowerment, taking responsibility, believing in your own capabilities, creative thinking and seeing things from a different perspective.

What represents the 'ham sandwich' that you are sick of eating?
What do you want instead of the ham sandwich?
What actions do you control?
What stops you from changing?
How could you bring about change?
Are you guilty of pointing the finger at all others except yourself?

32

INTRODUCTION

Last week I drove into a large multi-storey car park in the city. Having driven up to the barrier, a sign flashed that said, 'PRESS FOR TICKET', which I did. Immediately another sign flashed that said, 'THANK YOU. YOU MAY PROCEED'. I proceeded, and was then greeted with another sign, which read, 'TURN RIGHT'. I turned right and was then reminded to 'TAKE YOUR TICKET WITH YOU' which I dutifully did. Whilst waiting for the sign to tell me to 'HAVE A NICE LIFE', I was reminded of this story...

THE TALE

The Choice is Yours

Tired of talking to frustrated chief executives about their staff, who apparently refused to be 'empowered' and take on extra responsibility when required, and weary of listening to the woes of their staff who complained that everyone in the organization was a difficult person except *them*, I took myself off to a local Buddhist centre for some rest and recuperation.

Although since then I have been to the centre many times, this was my first visit. Not knowing much about Buddhism, and even less about the particular centre near York where I was heading, I had taken all the usual sensible precautions of writing a will, changing my house locks and leaving a forwarding address to friends and family in case I was whisked away, sold into slavery and never seen again.

On my arrival at the centre, I was immediately stunned by the peace, tranquillity and, indeed, the sheer size of the place. What is now known as The Madhyamaka Centre had originally been a privately-owned mansion dating back to Georgian times, and stood in some 40 acres of beautiful rolling hills, lakes and farm land.

I had arrived (typically) early for the weekend retreat. There were no other cars to be seen as I approached the grand marble pillars that flanked the main entrance to the mansion. Driving up to the entrance, I was immediately thrown into a quandary. Where were you supposed to park? Surely you couldn't park right next to the front doors. It seemed so presumptuous. No, there must be some special parking places reserved for 'weekend guests', 'people who had no idea what they were doing there' and other 'nobodies' like me.

Where was the warden with his white coat and clipboard to direct me to the right place? There were no signs, no lines and none of the guidance, rules or even orders that I had come to expect in situations of this sort.

While I was still pondering the issue, a young monk, dressed in the traditional Buddhist robes of maroon and saffron, who had been tending the garden nearby, saw me arrive and approached the car.

'Hello. Can I help you?' he asked smiling.

'Yes, I've come for the weekend retreat,' I replied. 'Can you tell me where I'm supposed to park?'

The young man put his hand to his chin, and surveyed the empty area around my car.

'Mmmmm, let me see...'

(I knew I'd come to the wrong place.)

Then he turned and looked in the other direction, shaking his head, '...or maybe...'

(I think I'll leave now before I'm abducted just for wrongful parking.)

Finally, the young monk looked back at me and by now with a definite twinkle in his eye, pointed at exactly the place where my car was standing and said, 'Here?!'

I wasn't expecting this. I was totally thrown.

'Oh. Is here all right, it's just... I didn't know... I haven't been before,' I stammered.

'Here is fine,' the young man said, smiling kindly, 'or there is more parking round the back of the building if you'd rather park there.'

'Oh, is that better?' I asked. 'I mean, would you rather I parked there? It's just I haven't been before and...' I burbled on.

The young man laughed. 'Here is fine. Round the back is fine. It's up to you. The choice is yours.'

With that he picked up his spade again and said, 'Would you excuse me? I need to get back to my work. I do hope you enjoy the weekend.'

I thanked him and remained motionless in my car as he walked away. *The choice is yours?* What did he mean? Couldn't he just *tell* me where to go? It would have been so much easier. Then if it turned out wrong, it would be his mistake.

Eventually, and after more deliberation, I made the decision to leave the car exactly where I had parked it in the first place, gathered my bags and walked towards the front door. As I did so, I saw the young monk who was by now totally engrossed again in digging his garden. And I couldn't help thinking – now *there* is a person who really knows what this empowerment thing is all about...

MORAL

If you made the right decision, the choice was yours. If you made the wrong decision, the choice was still yours.

REFLECTION

The story can be used to illustrate the real meaning of empowerment, in other words, that we must each take responsibility for our own actions. We cannot rely on other people to make decisions for us.

What do you and others in your organization understand by the term 'empowerment'?
Is empowerment seen as liberating – or frightening?
How empowered are you and people you know?
How could you – or others – take more responsibility for your own actions?
Does your organization really reward empowerment? In what way?
What happens if people make the 'wrong' decision?

33

INTRODUCTION

I have heard, amongst others, the motivational speaker Zig Ziglar tell this story. It serves as an illustration as to how blind and unthinking we are all capable of becoming from time to time, and how slavishly we tend to follow procedures and conventions, apparently giving up any independent thought. As the story shows, this type of mindless activity can be damaging – if not fatal!

THE TALE

The Processionary Caterpillars

There is a species of insect called the processionary caterpillar. It gets its name because of the strange behaviour it exhibits. The leader of the pack, in its quest for food, decides on a direction in which to walk, and all the others follow religiously and with complete conviction behind him. Observers of these peculiar creatures report that the followers are even known to half close their eyes, so blind and unquestioning is their faith in their leader, and so hypnotic and repetitive their activity. On and on they tramp, on their journey to...who knows where?

At the beginning of the last century, a French naturalist called Jean Henri Fabre studied the behaviour and instincts of insects like these, and looked particularly at any parallels that might exist between the human and insect mind. One of his most famous experiments was with a team of processionary caterpillars. He began the experiment by enticing the leader to walk round and round the edge of a large flowerpot. As expected, after a short time, all the other caterpillars in the troupe began to follow the leader. Round and round the flowerpot they went, apparently convinced that food was just round the corner – and completely oblivious to the juicy green leaves of the plant standing only inches above their heads. Amazingly, the little troupe kept up its fruitless search for food for several days, until eventually, through sheer exhaustion and hunger, one by one they started to drop off the edge.

In the end, most of the team died of starvation, even though there was sufficient food for all of them just inches away. They just couldn't see it was there.

MORAL

Follow my leader can be a dangerous game – particularly if you're not sure that the direction the leader is going in is the right one.

REFLECTION

You can use this story to illustrate and question the relationship between leader and led, and to discuss such topics as team empowerment, vision and creative thinking.

Fabre drew parallels between this behaviour and that of human beings. Was he right?
In what way are you, or others you know, like the processionary caterpillar?
How might you or others 'open your eyes' to what is going on around you?
Is your leader going in the right direction? Do you know what that direction is?
What is the 'food' that is inches away that you might not be seeing?
How could you persuade others to 'see' the food?
How will you get people to change direction if this is necessary?

34

INTRODUCTION

I have heard this story told by various speakers and read it in various formats, so its origin seems unclear. But it is a useful little tale for encouraging people to challenge their own and others' beliefs and capabilities.

THE TALE

The Elephant Story

If you have ever been to a circus or zoo you may wonder, when you see the elephant enclosure, why it is that the huge, old elephants that stand some 20 feet high and the tiny baby elephants, that only come up to your knees, are tethered with exactly the same size chain attached to a small stake in the ground.

You may think it completely illogical to treat these animals in the same way. Surely, you might argue, the older, larger elephant should have a much bigger and stronger chain than the baby one. A fully-grown elephant could, if it wanted to, simply walk away and, without even breaking into a sweat, pull the stake out of the ground, like you or I might pull up a daisy, or snap the chain like a twig.

But that's just the point. The old elephant has forgotten what it's like to struggle to be free. It learnt the lesson a long time ago, when it was a baby, that despite its efforts it remained imprisoned, and so, even though now, as a fully-grown adult, it might have the strength of 10 men, it believes itself to be just as much a prisoner – and has given up the struggle.

The baby elephant, who constantly pulls and tugs at its chain, still has the motivation to succeed – and the belief that it can.

MORAL

If you want to change your behaviour, first change your beliefs.

REFLECTION

This story can be used to discuss such issues as empowerment, beliefs and values, and 'freeing' yourself from constraints – real or imaginary.

In what way are you, or someone you know, like the old or baby elephant?
What represents the 'chain' that ties you down?
What would happen if you could free yourself?
Is there some situation in which you have given up the struggle?
What are your beliefs about your own capabilities? Do you need to change those beliefs in some way?
How will you rekindle the motivation to achieve?

35

INTRODUCTION

In Chapter 2 of the first part of this book, I talked about the need for rules and procedures in organizations and that having too many rules can stifle creativity and learning. Through coaching, I believe that you can identify and maximize people's experience, which might otherwise be lost. This is a good illustration of the problem!

THE TALE

Sticking to the Rules

Only this morning, whilst out for my morning walk and taking of the air, I met an elderly man walking his dog, who started telling me a story (unprompted by me, honestly) about how, after he had retired from his job as an engineer (having been with the same company for 35 years) his successor had apparently cost the company in the region of £12 million. It was all because of a simple mistake, which he admitted he and his colleagues had made many times while they were there.

I was intrigued by the story, so I asked him, 'So, how come it cost the company that amount of money when your successor made the mistake, and nothing when you did it?'

The man smiled knowingly. 'If my colleagues and I had still been there, we would simply have wedged a piece of wood in the machine to stop it running,' he told me, and then sighed resignedly. 'Still, that's *rules* for you.'

'Oh I see,' I said (not really seeing) and then asked naïvely, 'Is that what it tells you to do in the rule book?'

I had obviously been set up to ask just the 'right' type of stupid question, because my companion roared with laughter, and said, 'No! That's the whole point. It's NOT in the rule book. It's in here,' he said, pointing to his head. 'You can't run a place like that by the rule book. People's experience is what keeps the place going. Of course, we could have taught that guy what to do before we left, but,' he chuckled, 'nobody thought to ask us to do it.'

MORAL

The rule book can't teach us everything.

REFLECTION

You can use this story to explore the use of rules and procedures, independent and creative thought, valuing the power of experience and personal empowerment.

What rules or procedures exist in your organization?
Do the rules help or hinder creativity and empowerment?
Are there some procedures that need revising?
How do people learn in your organization?
How is experience valued?
What stops you, or others, from changing?
How could you encourage more innovation?

36

INTRODUCTION

I heard Rosabeth Moss Kanter, an expert on change management, tell this true story in the United States a couple of years ago. She was giving a speech about empowerment, and the fact that all of us have the need to feel we have some form of power and be in control of our lives. In people's working lives, it is easy, if swamped by rules and procedures, to become disempowered – as this story demonstrates.

THE TALE

Stamp Out Creativity!

I went into my local Post Office to buy some stamps.

'Twenty stamps please,' I said to the man behind the counter.

'Sorry,' the man replied, 'I can't help you. I don't have enough stamps for that.'

'Oh well, never mind,' I replied, 'I'll take whatever you have. How many stamps do you have?'

'Twenty-five,' the man replied.

I wondered whether he was being facetious, but one look at his face told me otherwise.

'Twenty-five?' I echoed incredulously. 'But I said I only want twenty.'

'I know,' said the man 'I'm sorry but I have to keep twenty-five stamps in stock at all times. I can't sell you any.'

'But why do you need to keep twenty-five stamps?' I asked, getting even more annoyed.

'No idea,' said the man with a resigned air. 'Those are the rules.'

MORAL

Rosabeth Moss Kanter says, 'It is powerless-ness, not power, that ultimately corrupts.' If people have no other way of demonstrating power, they become controlling of little, inconsequential things in life – like stamps!

REFLECTION

You can use this anecdote to discuss such issues as personal empowerment and disempowerment, taking responsibility, creative thinking and
the use of rules and procedures.

*Can you relate this story to your own working situation – or someone you
know?*
Are there rules and procedures in place that are meaningless?
Do you and people you work with understand the rules and procedures?
How could you encourage people to think more autonomously at work?
How could you bring about the change?

37

INTRODUCTION

A friend of mine was recently watching a television programme that featured a number of entrepreneurs talking about their achievements. 'That's nothing new,' he said, tutting to himself. 'I could have done that.' 'Yes,' I said, 'but the difference is, they did it and you didn't.' We all could write a book, or start a business, or become a millionaire. But it takes courage in your own convictions to see an idea through – and it involves risk. Valerie Stewart tells this story.

THE TALE

Empowerment Involves Risk

Recently I worked with a group of people from the personnel function of a large company in dire trouble. We were working on a plan for the personnel department's contribution to getting the organization out of the mire. They worked hard and well, and put together a splendid presentation for the group personnel director's arrival on Friday. They had a plan to bust the bureaucracy, make innovation easier, get back in touch with the customer, reduce interdepartmental fights and give up a lot of their own power. It wouldn't have been the total salvation of the company, but it would surely have helped.

The personnel director sat through it all, and then responded, 'I can see the sense of what you say, and if you can prove to me now that it stands a 95 per cent chance of working, I'll give it serious consideration', thus demonstrating the low-risk, anti-innovation attitude that had got them into trouble in the first place. They packed up, and started reading the job adverts in the *Daily Telegraph* and preparing their résumés.

(From *The David Solution* by Valerie Stewart, 1990, Gower.
Reproduced with permission of Gower Publishing Limited.)

MORAL

There is less risk in criticizing others than in doing it yourself – and, of course, less gain!

REFLECTION

You can use this story to discuss such issues as personal empowerment, taking risk and responsibility, believing in your own capabilities and creative thinking.

Can you relate this story to your own situation or someone you know?
What have you been afraid of doing because it involved risk?
What would you do if there was no risk at all?
What stops you, or others, from making changes?
How could you 'bust the bureaucracy' in your organization?
How could you support people's creative ideas more?

38

INTRODUCTION

Many people say 'it can't be done' and then go on to behave in a way that is consistent with their beliefs. This true story might help some people to see their beliefs in a different light.

THE TALE

The Four-Minute Mile

In 1954, Roger Bannister, a British physician and athlete, ran a mile in three minutes and 59.4 seconds. By modern-day standards, this might not seem a great achievement. But at the time, the significance of this was that, not only was this was a new world record, but it also shattered the belief that had been strongly held up until that time that it was not humanly possible for any man to run a mile in less than four minutes.

Ironically, less than two months later, Roger Bannister's record was broken by an Australian athlete, John Landy, who ran the mile in 3 minutes 58 seconds. Since then the record has been bettered many times. But it was Roger Bannister who opened the door for many other athletes by proving that your beliefs can change the world.

MORAL

There is danger in being negatively influenced by other people's beliefs.

REFLECTION

You can use this story to discuss such issues as how beliefs can affect your behaviour and how to believe in your own capabilities.

What is represented by the 'four-minute mile' that nobody believes can be achieved?
Have you been influenced by other people? In what way?
Are your beliefs holding you back in some way?
Are there any beliefs that you might want to change? How could you change them?
What effect would this change have on your life?

39

INTRODUCTION

From a very early age we all start to have beliefs about ourselves, and whether these beliefs are positive or negative can have a powerful effect on our behaviour. It doesn't actually make any difference in our minds whether these beliefs are true; if we think they are true then we behave accordingly. You've heard the expression 'ignorance is bliss' I'm sure, and this was certainly the case in this next story.

THE TALE

Seeing Through the Glasses

Some time ago, we celebrated Guy Fawkes night. For those who haven't heard of him, he was the chap who on 5 November 1605 attempted – and failed rather spectacularly – to blow up the Houses of Parliament in London. Not one normally to commemorate the occasion, I took a whim on this year to have a bonfire and some fireworks and, having made the discovery that two meagre-looking rockets would set me back the cost of a small house (it was never like that in my day!), some friends kindly offered – in exchange for food and wine – to come round and share their fireworks with us (making a total of four meagre rockets).

Their two children, Dafyd aged 11 and Martina aged 14, who I hadn't met before, were charming young people, and after we had all enjoyed the fireworks (which didn't take long!) and our meal, we sat down to share jokes, stories, and other party tricks.

Steve, one of our friends, was prevailed upon to do his party piece. Now this is a trick that I have seen him and my husband do many times over the last 20 years, and I'm going to describe it now, so I just hope I don't get ostracized by the Magic Circle. Anyway, the trick consists of Steve assembling a number of drinking glasses on a table and pretending to identify which drinking glass has been touched by someone while he is out of the room. This trick requires that you have a 'plant' in the audience (in this case my husband), who obligingly folds his arms, blows his nose, or makes another subtle movement every time you touch the right glass. I'm sorry to disappoint you but there is no magic in this trick whatsoever.

The performance between the two was executed with its normal panache, and the children were all suitably impressed. Dafyd, who I'm sure in later life will turn into a *real* performer, insisted on having a go at the trick. His announcement threw us all into something of a dilemma –

how do you tell a child that there is no way he could possibly succeed because basically the whole thing was a sham?

While the adults sat looking pessimistically at each other, knowing what was to come, Dafyd left the room, and one of the other children touched a glass. He duly came back, and after much deliberation and dramatics *and* to everyone's astonishment – chose the right one! Now, you might say that that in itself was not that amazing – except he went on to do the trick three times, and each time he chose the right glass! Intrigued, I said to Dafyd, 'That was brilliant! How did you do that?'

'I don't know. *I suppose I just have the power,*' he replied confidently and rather melodramatically.

Since that night, I have thought about Dafyd and the trick quite a bit, and I still can't work out how he did it. I can only draw the conclusion that he succeeded because nobody told him it was impossible – a belief that Guy Fawkes possibly could have benefited from all those years ago.

MORAL

If you believe that you can – you're right, and if you believe that you can't – you're still right.

REFLECTION

You can use this story to discuss such issues as beliefs and their effects on people's behaviour, personal empowerment and creative thinking.

What 'empowering' beliefs do you, or someone you know, have?
What limiting beliefs do you have?
How do these beliefs affect the way you do things?
Do you need to review some of your beliefs? How will you change them?
What things would you do if you knew you could not fail?

40

INTRODUCTION

It's amazing how quickly people become indoctrinated with 'the way we do it' in organizations, just in the same way that people in hospitals, schools or prisons can become institutionalized. This story is a reminder of how easily it can happen to all of us.

THE TALE

Walls

A young man I was coaching some years ago had been charged by his manager to investigate ways of improving the workflow within the manufacturing company where he was team leader. He had set about the project in good consultative management style, by designing a questionnaire and asking a number of his colleagues for their views. He confessed to me that his own recommendation would be to knock down some of the existing internal walls in order to leave a bigger, open-plan area. This would mean that machinery could be better positioned to make the workflow more efficient and, in addition, it would leave more room for future expansion of the factory.

He spent a long time drawing a scaled plan of the area in question, his idea being to then photocopy this and circulate it to his colleagues to get their views. He sketched in only the outer perimeter of the building, hoping to give his colleagues free reign with their ideas.

To his astonishment he discovered that when the copies were returned from his colleagues, the first thing each one had done was to meticulously draw all the internal walls back in.

MORAL

Are you imagining walls that do not exist?

REFLECTION

You can use this story to discuss such issues as limiting beliefs and their effects on people's behaviour, and creative thinking.

What 'walls' are you, or someone you know, imagining in life?
Why are these walls there?
What would happen if the walls were not there? What could you do that you can't do now?
What stops you from knocking down the walls?
Who could help you?

Success and Self-Esteem

'I Told You That You Could Do It!'

One of the most common things that holds people back in their own development is a feeling of low self-esteem and this hopefully inspiring set of stories will encourage people to believe in themselves – their greatest resource!

41

INTRODUCTION

A business colleague told me this tale years ago, and indeed it's so long ago that I've forgotten the chap's name! (That's boosted his ego!) But I always remember saying to him that if I wrote a book on self-esteem or personal development, I'd call it 'I like your socks' because I thought it was such a good title. Well, naming a story in a book is the next best thing! I use this to illustrate some of the dangers and pitfalls in giving and receiving feedback.

THE TALE

I Like Your Socks!

Some years ago, a colleague and I were discussing the dubious pleasures and benefits gained from various personal development training courses that we had been on over the years, principally from the 'let's knock them down and then build them back up again' school of training. Although it had started as a serious discussion (well, mostly), we ended up vying for who could name the course that had had the daftest and most embarrassing exercises. (Come on, you've all done it!)

My friend started laughing. 'I remember one,' he said. 'I worked for this organization, and we'd all been sent on a team-building course, to see if we could work together more productively. Well, there was this guy in the department, a senior manager, let's call him Gerald, that no one could stand, and I wondered how people would deal with him. One of the first exercises we were given was where everyone milled around in a circle, and we had paper Post-it notes stuck to our backs. Everyone had to think of something complimentary to say about each of their colleagues and go up and write it on the person's back. At the end of the exercise, we were all supposed to get together and share our feelings about what had been written, whether we agreed with it and so on.

Well, after a while most people had at least one or two complimentary notes written on their backs, all fairly innocuous observations like "you've got a good sense of humour", "you're very good with customers" and "you have a nice smile". But not Gerald. His back was a "compliment-free zone". Eventually, and I think more out of pity and embarrassment than anything else, one of our administrative assistants went up and wrote something on his back. We were all really curious as to what it was. When I could get a chance I went up to have a look. She'd written in big letters "I like your socks".'

My friend finished by saying, 'I'm not sure whether that comment was better or worse than not having anything at all. But we were never sent on any more training courses after that!'

MORAL

If you can't say something nice, don't say anything at all!

REFLECTION

This story can be used to discuss such issues as self-esteem, praise and reward, giving and receiving feedback and people's perceptions of others.

How do you give and receive feedback in your organization?
In what context is feedback given? Is it objective?
Is feedback given publicly or privately? Which do you think is better?
Do you give and/or receive praise in your organization?
In what ways could the praise you give or receive be more meaningful?

42

INTRODUCTION

There used to be a time when I thought it a sign of weakness to admit that I didn't know or understand. But I've since learnt that in fact it takes more strength to do just that rather than remain silent. And you usually find if you admit your igno- rance, there will be many others who will thank you – because they didn't under- stand either!

THE TALE

KNC Consulting

David King, Head of King Manufacturing Plc, was obsessed with imple- menting new systems and procedures. Forms, flow charts, formulae, maps, models and methodology – he had the lot! He had no idea how most of them worked, mind you, but he loved them anyway.

So all-consuming was this obsession that the day-to-day running of King Manufacturing tended to get overlooked, as David continued his constant quest to find the latest and most fashionable system. He had been known to sulk for days if he learnt that one of his competitors had implemented a system that he hadn't heard of. And you could be sure that, two or three weeks later, King Manufacturing would have a new set of consultants in the boardroom, complete with high-tech presentations and flip chart pads. And, sure enough, two or three months later, the bills would come rolling in – hundreds and thousands of pounds of company money – and nothing much else to show.

The long-suffering board of directors at King Manufacturing were used to David's behaviour. They would shake their heads and groan when another 'flavour of the month concept' came onto the market, knowing that, at best, it would cost the company dear and at worst it would cause them more work and worry. But they also knew that there was no point in arguing; David's obsession would stand no argument.

Needless to say, news spread of David King not, as he would like to think, because of his visionary thinking or his generous work with chari- ties, but more as a result of his vanity, stubbornness and apparent lack of caution when it came to spending company money. Among those to hear were two unscrupulous business consultants who were a bit down on their luck and had just happened to come into the town.

'Hello,' they said to each other, 'there's a nice little pot of gold to be made here.' Having quickly put together a bogus business plan and marketing strategy and designed a completely fictitious computer Web site, they felt they were ready to approach David King.

Calling themselves KNC© Consulting Associates (no one knew what KNC stood for, but were embarrassed to ask, thinking that they should know), and with a 'revolutionary and powerful computerized system, specially designed to maximize your profitability and growth – visit us on www.cons@knc.co.uk/consulting', they soon procured an invitation to meet David at King Manufacturing's site. They had, of course, taken the precaution of having with them a sheaf of testimonials from satisfied customers, all of which were self-penned.

'Well, these are all well and good,' David mused as he looked through the letters, 'but I was looking for something *really* different that none of our competitors has had.' Then he added, 'I am hoping for ' "Business-man of the Year" award this year, you know.'

The two unscrupulous consultants were ready for this.

'Absolutely,' said one.

'We hear where you're coming from David,' said the other.

'And in fact, we have saved the best till last to run past you. We have just recently invented a business process auditing system, but...' they added, smiling smugly to each other, 'it is *so* sophisticated that when it is printed out it is only visible to those who are the most intelligent and knowledgeable in your company. A lesser person, let's say, an administrative assistant, cleaner or finance accountant, *will not be able to see a thing.* As well as being the most unique system in the world, it is also a powerful assessment tool for people in your company. You will be immediately able to differentiate between the wise and the foolish.'

Needless to say, David was thrilled. 'Start customizing the system for me straight away, and I will present the concept at the next Board meeting in June.'

The two consultants, having demanded a large sum of money in advance on the pretext of buying software and employing computer programmers, went away and duly set up their desks and computers in a room that David had provided for them. All day long, the computers went 'whirr-whirr' and the printers went 'clickety-click', for the consultants had to maintain the illusion. Secretly, they were just sitting in a corner, playing solitaire and whiling away their time.

After a week, David, who was getting impatient but was slightly nervous of the assessment element of the system, not wanting to appear a fool, said to his Finance Director, 'Go to the consultants' room and see how they are getting on with my system, then report back to me on their progress.'

The Finance Director did as he was told and went to see the consul-tants from KNC©. They told him about their invention and particularly its powerful assessment properties and invited him in to inspect their work. But, of course, when he looked at the paper being churned out of the printers, he could see nothing but thin air. The Finance Director was very shocked but, not wanting to appear a fool, feigned delight.

'Why, this is the most exquisite and complex system I have ever seen!' he enthused. 'I can't wait to report back to David.'

Another week went by and David, growing even more impatient but still slightly nervous of the assessment element, sent his Manufacturing Director to inspect progress. When he looked at the computers, he too could see nothing but thin air. He was very worried. 'I must not let David know that I am not fit to do my job,' he thought. So, like his colleague, not wanting to appear a fool, he exclaimed, 'I have never in my life seen anything so brilliant!'

The day of the Board meeting finally arrived and the two fake consultants, with great pomp and ceremony, presented the KNC© system, duly customized 'to meet the particular and specific demands of King Manufacturing'. Sheaf after sheaf of totally blank paper was laid out on the huge boardroom table.

'My word!' said David, who was totally shocked that he too could see nothing, particularly when apparently all his Directors could. 'Well, well, well,' he mused, not wanting to appear a fool, but not being able to think of any other appropriate comment.

'Why, it's amazing!' said all the Directors in unison, watching David like hawks and following his lead.

While they were standing admiring the consultants' supposed handiwork, a young man who was carrying out a school project at King Manufacturing walked into the room, and wondering what all the fuss was about, looked over one of the Director's shoulders. He too saw the blank sheets of paper spread out on the table.

'But it's got nothing on,' he said simply.

'Oh, hark at him,' laughed David. 'Now this is why you're learning from the likes of me. You couldn't possibly be expected to see and make sense of such a sophisticated system.'

'Well, it might be sophisticated,' said the innocent, 'but there's still nothing on that paper.'

With that, all the other Directors, knowing it to be true, started to join in a similar chorus.

'I didn't think there was anything there...'

'We didn't like to say...'

'Not wanting to appear a fool...'

That same day, the two bogus consultants from KNC© Consulting Associates were removed from the building.

'By the way,' said one of David's colleagues, 'what did KNC stand for?'

'No idea,' replied David truthfully. 'But you know there might have been something in their system. I was reading about this new concept the other day…'

MORAL

It takes courage to understand – but even more to admit that you don't!

REFLECTION

This story (or of course in its original format of *The King's New Clothes* by Hans Christian Andersen) can be used to discuss such issues as self-confidence, believing in your own capability, learning, understanding and using jargon.

Do you know a KNC© Consulting or equivalent? (Let's hope not!)
How closely do you work with partners, consultants and so forth in your organization?
What are you afraid to ask? Why are you afraid to ask it?
What should you admit that you don't know?
What would happen if you admit you don't know?
How can you keep communication simple and uncomplicated in your organization?

43

INTRODUCTION

The life story of Hans Christian Andersen, who wrote the original version of The Ugly Duckling, *sounds like it could have been taken from one of his own tales! Born into a very poor family, he suffered considerable hardship as a child and was bullied at school, before eventually being sponsored to take a degree at Copenhagen University. This retold and shortened version of the original can serve as a powerful metaphor for coachees who are looking to address issues of self-esteem.*

THE TALE

The Ugly Duckling

Once upon a time there was an ugly duckling. He knew he was ugly because his friends used to laugh and stare at him whenever he walked by. He knew he was ugly because he had heard his parents comparing him – not very favourably – to his brothers and sisters. They were little and cute and fluffy and he was tall and gangly with a great long neck and a funny-looking beak. He was different – and he hated it.

He was born in the summertime, which was a lovely time in the country. The wheat was golden and all the grass and the leaves on the trees were a rich, luscious green. It was warm and sunny in the farmyard as the mother duck proudly paraded her new brood. But the other ducks and hens in the yard took one look at the ugly duckling and said, 'What sort of a duckling is *that*? He's so big and ugly – he's got to be a turkey with legs like that!'

They pushed and pulled and kicked the poor ugly duckling from one corner of the farmyard to the other, until he could stand it no longer and he ran straight out of the farmyard, over the hedge and across the green fields to the next village.

'They hate me because I'm so ugly,' cried the poor duckling, as he continued to run. He ran and ran until he came to a huge marsh where the wild ducks lived, and there he hid for a long time. When the wild ducks eventually discovered him, they gathered round him and said, 'What sort of a bird are you? You're not one of *us*, that's for sure. Now run along; there's another marsh just over that hill. You'll probably fit in better there; they're not so…uh…choosy.'

Laughing and joking with each other, they kicked and jostled the ugly duckling out of the marsh and up the hill.

'Maybe they're right,' said the poor duckling to himself as he toiled up the hill. 'Maybe I'll fit in better somewhere else.'

Just with that, he heard a sudden '*bang!*' in the air above him and, to his horror, realized that he was in the middle of a shooting party – and the main target appeared to be *him*! He ran and ran until he found some thick reeds on the edge of the water where he hid for a long time until the hunters seemed to lose interest and move away.

'They're shooting at me because I'm so ugly,' said the poor creature to himself. And he set off again, across fields and hills and meadows. On and on he trudged, and by now it was approaching autumn and there was a strong wind picking up, which made it increasingly difficult for the little creature to make his way.

One day, just as it was getting dark, he came to a ramshackle cottage at the edge of a wood. He was so cold and tired and hungry he thought he would search for food and warmth inside. Quietly, hoping not to disturb anyone, the ugly duckling crept in through a crack in the door. But as he did so, he woke up the old woman who lived in the cottage with her cat and her hen.

'What on earth is *that*?' she shrieked, chasing the duckling round the room and swatting him with her broom handle.

The cat, who was the master of the house (or thought he was) pinned the duckling to the wall and said, 'We might make some use of you...do you lay eggs?'

'I don't know,' said the duckling fearfully, 'but I can take a crack at it.'

They kept him on trial for three weeks, but at the end of that time, when no eggs appeared, the old woman kicked him out of the cottage. 'Be off with you, you useless creature.'

'Maybe she's right,' thought the ugly duckling to himself as he ran off again. 'Maybe I am useless. I don't seem to fit in with my own kind, and I didn't fit in with the cat and the hen either. There must be *someone* in the world who understands me,' he said sadly, as the rain started to pour and he started to sniffle. 'I will go out into the wide world and seek my real family.'

Off he went again, over hills and down valleys, across fields and through villages. By now it was nearly winter and the weather was becoming bitterly cold. After some time of wandering, the duckling found a lake to swim on, which raised his spirits a little, but he found, as winter progressed, that he had to keep swimming all the time just to stop the water from freezing. During the day he picked up what bits of food he could from the fields and the roadside and any crumbs left by passers-by in the villages. All through the winter he lived in this miserable way.

But eventually the spring came, the ice began to melt and the sun began to shine again, and the duckling, who had been lying exhausted at the side of the lake, raised his wings and started to flap, with more strength than he had felt for a long time. As he stretched and looked around him, he saw at the other side of the lake three beautiful birds gliding towards him. He knew that they were swans, and thinking that he would rather be abused and beaten by them than by the other ducks and hens or by the old woman and her cat, he started swimming towards them. But, just as he bowed his head, expecting the worst, he suddenly caught sight of his own reflection in the waters of the lake. To his amazement, it was no longer the tall and gangly creature with a great long neck and a funny looking beak that looked back at him. He realized that he was just like these other birds – he was a swan, too!

As the other birds swam up to greet him, the young swan thought of all the hardships that he had experienced in the last year when he was an 'ugly duckling' and how happy he was now. 'I wonder...' he thought, as he looked at the beautiful birds gathered around him, 'if they were ugly ducklings, too?'

MORAL

We can all be ugly ducklings or beautiful swans – it all depends on your point of view!

REFLECTION

This story can be used to discuss such issues as self-esteem, self-image, confidence and identity.

Do you think of yourself as an ugly duckling? Do any people that you know think of themselves as ugly ducklings?
How will you become the beautiful swan?
When will this happen? Has it happened already without you noticing?
Is your self-image accurate?
Who would give you a constructive and objective view?

44

INTRODUCTION

I was shocked to discover that something like 80 per cent of the things we typically say to ourselves (internal dialogue) are negative. No one really yet understands why we try to sabotage ourselves in this way, but it is something about which we need to be aware. Just think – if we spoke to our friends in the same way we do ourselves we wouldn't have many friends left!

THE TALE

Did You Pass?

Some 10 years ago, I took my first practitioner course in Neurolinguistic Programming (NLP) with a training organization in the north of England. One thing that I learnt during the course was that I (along with many of my peers, I suspect) had a fairly active, and it has to be said, pretty negative 'internal dialogue'. This is the NLP term for that little nagging inner voice, you know, the one that sounds a bit like your mother on a bad day, and says such things as: 'I can't believe you could be so stupid', 'Well, you've messed up there again, haven't you?' or 'That's just typical of you – you always get it wrong!'

Hearing messages such as this on a regular basis is at best not particularly helpful and at worst potentially damaging to one's self-esteem and level of confidence.

After several months on the course, the final day of the assessment arrived. All participants were put through a series of tests and activities, and although, like any type of assessment, the process was a bit nerve-racking, I thought I had probably managed to pass – just.

The procedure was that at the end of the day each of us went in turn for a private audience with our trainer and one of her assistants on the course, in order to receive 'the judgement' on our performance.

Eventually it was my turn. I knocked nervously.

'Come in.' I heard a voice from the other side of the door.

I walked in and sat down on the chair that was positioned in front of the two trainers.

'Well…' said my teacher, with what I felt sure was a resigned sigh. I expected the worst. '*Did you pass?*'

It took a minute or two for her question to sink in. 'Pardon?' This was not the sort of 'feedback' I had been expecting.

'Did you deserve to pass?' her assistant joined in.

Their questions threw me completely. 'I...uh...think so, well, that is, I suppose...um...' I floundered.

'The point is,' continued the first, with a twinkle in her eye, 'WE know that you've been successful on the course. But what we wanted to find out was – *do YOU know that you're successful?'*

It's a question I still ponder...

MORAL

Is your inner voice on your side – or somebody else's?

REFLECTION

This story can be used to discuss such issues as self-esteem, success, reward and recognition, and feedback.

What is your inner voice saying?
What type of language do you use with yourself – positive or negative?
Is this language healthy and helpful?
How could you make the inner voice more helpful to your future?
How will you change?
What type of inner voice do other people have?

45

INTRODUCTION

I hear so many coaches trying to 'encourage' (that's coaching jargon for 'push') their coachees into achieving a goal that was never theirs in the first place. Not everyone is capable of or indeed wants to be 'top dog'. This is a wonderful example, from Jim Cathcart, of how not to coach!

THE TALE

The Acorn Principle

The acorn principle states that your greatest, fastest and easiest growth always comes from your natural abilities. The source of the acorn metaphor is that most people tend to look at other people as if they can change them into whatever they want. What they ought to be doing is looking within those people to see what kind of seed is on the inside. Just like a tree, every person has a seed.

A lot of managers get it backwards. They look at that little acorn that they see inside somebody, and they say, 'Acorn, I think you have potential. I think with a little training and a little hard work, you could be a giant redwood.' In fact, the only thing an acorn is going to be is an oak, but it could be a wonderful one if you developed it right.

Then this misled manager comes back and says, 'Acorn, here's what I'm going to do for you. I'm going to work with you to help develop your redwood skills. Here's a tape I want you to listen to called *The Power of Positive Redwood Thinking* by Dr Norman Vincent Tree. Here's a book on the history of some of the great redwoods of all time. Learn from their example. I'd also like you to start networking with redwoods. Just take a redwood to lunch, find out what they're like and ask them their secrets. I also want you to say a daily affirmation I've written for you. It says, "I am a redwood, great and tall. My mighty branches shelter all. I'm good enough, I'm smart enough and, doggone it, people like me".'

Now I ask you, what's that acorn going to be when it grows up? You're probably thinking an oak. I say, yes, but a really insecure oak – because all this time it has been getting the message that it wasn't OK to be who and what it was. It has been getting the message that it ought to be something else and in this case something it is not capable of becoming.

But what if that same manager takes a different approach and says, 'First let me find out what is the nature of this person.' Then come the other questions, 'How can I cultivate that nature?', 'How can I find the natural gifts that this person has and then structure a growth plan around those natural gifts?' Then they might have said to the acorn, 'Here's a tape on *The Power of Positive Oak Thinking*. Here are some examples of successful oaks I'd like you to learn from. Here's a sign-up for a seminar on oak skills. I want you to start networking with other oaks, and I've written an affirmation for you that is related to your oak qualities.'

If they had done that, the use of the same techniques would have paid off handsomely because they were nurturing the nature that was already there. The more we find the seeds that are inside ourselves and other people, the more we will value those persons as they are and help them grow along their natural lines so that they tap their true potential.

(From 'The acorn principle' by Jim Cathcart, in *Heart at Work*, 1996, ed J Canfield, McGraw-Hill, New York. Reproduced with the permission of The McGraw-Hill Companies.)

MORAL

To thine own self be true.

REFLECTION

This story can be used to discuss such issues as self-esteem, personal growth, goal setting and identity.

Are you, or someone you know, an oak – or a giant redwood?
What are your natural abilities?
How could you discover more of the natural abilities of others? How might you nurture those abilities?
Are you guilty of 'overdeveloping' people?
Has someone forced you into achieving a goal that wasn't really yours?

46

INTRODUCTION

I was fortunate to go to Bangkok many years ago. I thought it was a wonderful city. It is a city full of colour, smell – and noise! It made a nice peaceful change to visit some of the many temples there. This true tale is all about secrets and hidden treasure, and I'm sure Bangkok has hundreds of those!

THE TALE

The Hidden Gold

In Bangkok there is a temple called Wat Trai Mitre, where the now famous statue called the Gold Buddha sits. For those who haven't seen it, it is a stunning statue, made of solid gold and standing all of seven feet high.

But its appearance was not always as it is now. Many years ago, the statue was dull and completely covered in plaster, and its true composition only came to light because a monk noticed that the statue was peeling in places and suggested that it be cleaned and restored.

It was only when they came to examine the place where the plaster had come away that they noticed a glint of something yellow and shiny. Further examination showed that what the monks had in their possession, was not, as they thought, an ordinary plaster Buddha of very little worth, but actually a statue that was made of solid gold. It is believed that the monks had camouflaged the statue many years ago with a thin layer of plaster to protect it from looters and pillagers.

So the Gold Buddha of Bangkok was restored to its present-day glory. And if you see it today, you will notice its serene and majestic face still wearing its beatific smile: the keeper, for all those years, of a wonderful secret.

MORAL

You can't always judge a book by its cover.

REFLECTION

This story can be used to discuss such issues as self-esteem, hidden talents, latent skills and confidence.

Are you, or someone you know, hiding a golden quality?
Why is this gold hidden from view?
What would happen if the gold were revealed?
What would it take to reveal the treasure within?
What talents or skills do other people have that they don't recognize?
How could you help others reveal their worth?

47

INTRODUCTION

Those of you who have read my first book, Tales for Trainers, *might remember the story of 'The Enormous Turnip', which many people told me was one of their favourite tales. In case you haven't read it, it is a traditional 'cumulative' tale, which describes how a man and a woman, her granddaughter, a dog, a cat and finally a mouse, work together effectively to pull up a turnip. The final line is 'and that night, they all had a delicious meal of turnip – and the mouse sat at the head of the table'. I am indebted to Dave Clarke, a friend of mine, who felt inspired to write a sequel!*

THE TALE

EnorMouse Moves On

After the Awfully Big Adventure with the old man and woman, her grand-daughter, dog, cat and the turnip, the mouse went travelling.

Wherever he went, Enor proudly told his story, and at first his listeners were charmed and cheered by the outcome. But after a while they became bored with the same story told again and again, especially when, in the retelling, it became obvious that the mouse thought that he alone was responsible for the success. Soon nobody at all believed his claims of being the 'Best Turnip Puller in Town', and they laughed as they said, 'How can anybody of your stature make any difference?'

As the months went by, and the derisory comments took their hold, Enor, too, began to doubt the value of his own contribution.

So, one day, feeling bad, feeling sad, he returned home to his village, and lay down in the long grass at the side of the Green. It was annual fête, day, and everyone was having a jolly time, dancing, singing and playing games. You may think that Enor was watching events at the fête, but actually he was thinking once again of the last time he had been there, and how great it had felt to be part of that successful team. And how lonely he felt now.

Suddenly he realized that right in front of him were the old man and woman, granddaughter, dog and cat, and, would you believe it, they were pulling (unsuccessfully) in the Tug of War competition. As they returned for their final pull, they saw him in the long grass, and with a cry said, 'Oh, Enor, it's *you!* You're the very person we need to complete our team. Join us, do!'

They rushed towards him and enfolded him in a group hug. Enor was thrilled at the recognition and began to remember the pleasures of being part of a team, rather than a lone player. He whispered shyly, slyly smiling though his whiskers, 'All right…let's go pull some turnip!'

That made them all laugh, and, remembering their last successful efforts together, they turned confidently to pick up the rope.

MORAL

Celebrate team success and recognize that individual contributions from all are still needed.

REFLECTION

This story can be used to discuss such issues as achieving success both individually and as a team, building self-esteem, effective team work, and reward and recognition.

Are all of your team members rewarded for success?
In what way is team success celebrated?
Is there a 'mouse' in your team?
Has one person been singled out for reward rather than the whole team? Was this fair?
What previous successes can your team draw from to build for the future?

48

INTRODUCTION

The technique of using 'affirmations', that is, statements you say to yourself to help in potentially difficult situations and to build your own feelings of confidence and calm, has become more commonly used in the last ten years or so, and there's no doubt that the technique can be a powerful one – both positive and negative. It all depends on precisely what you say…

THE TALE

Red Necks

I was working with a senior manager in the south of England. She had a number of important presentations to give to customers and wanted to improve her presentation skills. During our coaching sessions I had been extolling the virtues of being prepared, focusing on breathing from the diaphragm – *and* talking positively to yourself.

'That's all well and good,' she said rather impatiently. 'But it's not giving the presentation that's the problem, it's just I get so nervous and…' She paused, as if for me to appreciate the true sense of occasion and gravity, and then said with some feeling '…I get The Red Neck.'

It sounded like a fatal disease the way she described it, but I knew what she meant, and I'm sure you do, too. What she was referring to was the way in which some individuals' necks and faces can seem to take on a life of their own, and start to develop a red mottled effect, a bit like a huge nettle rash. This is, of course, purely a reaction to stress, the old 'fight or flight' syndrome of which we are all aware, but it doesn't help us particularly when we are trying to pretend that we are cool and in control.

'And it's no good talking to me about affirmations,' she continued, almost defiantly. 'I've tried them and they don't work.'

Curious, I asked, 'Tell me, what *exactly* do you say to yourself?'

Confidently and without hesitation, she said, 'I must *not* get a red neck. I must *not* get a red neck.'

'And what happens then?' I asked.

'I get a red neck,' she said in a resigned tone.

Well, there's a surprise! Of course, what the woman was doing, quite unwittingly, was reinforcing what she *didn't* want, and actually telling her brain to deliver a *red neck*. One thing we know about affirmations is that, for them to work properly, they have to follow what I call the '3Ps' –

'Personal, Positive and Present tense'. For example, '*I, Margaret, am now calm and dealing positively with my emotions.*'

If you are one of those people who try to give up something by telling yourself that you don't want a *cream cake*, that you shouldn't have a *large glass of wine* and you really don't want another *cigarette* – I'm afraid you are doomed to failure. Come back! I haven't finished the story...

Curiously, as the woman was describing her red neck to me, what do you think started to happen? Yes, you guessed it! She got a red neck! And it was increasingly difficult, while I continued to talk to her, watching the rash spread rapidly towards the top of her head, not to look at it, burst out laughing and say, 'Oh my God! You're right. Isn't that dreadful?!'

But of course I'm far too sensitive to do something like that. So I've just written about it instead.

THE MORAL

Some of us can be our own worst enemy. Be careful that your internal voice is on your side!

REFLECTION

You can use this cautionary tale to coach people in how to use affirmations correctly, the power of positive thinking, and so forth.

What affirmations are you using? Do they work?
Are you sabotaging yourself unwittingly by using negative language?
Never use 'I must not...' in your affirmation statement.
In what stressful situations could you use affirmations?
Be careful who you share your affirmations with – not everyone will share your enthusiasm!

49

INTRODUCTION

I always find myself in something of a moral dilemma in balancing the theories of assertiveness with the notion of cherishing others. While working on a management project with an airport in the north of England, I was educated in this dilemma by one of my course attendees – and I am grateful for his candour in the matter.

THE TALE

The Firemen's Rule

I was working with a group of managers from an airport in the north of England. Part of the training course required some one-to-one coaching with individuals. During one of the sessions, I got into discussion with a young fireman on the notion of influencing skills – passive, assertive and aggressive – and how he related to other people.

He asked me, 'What do you suppose is the first rule of fire-fighting?'

I thought for a moment. 'Well, I suppose the main purpose of the job must be…to save people's lives?' I answered, with a question in my voice.

'You might think so,' said my wise companion, 'but you'd be wrong. The first rule they teach you when you're training to be a fireman is "save yourself".'

While I was mulling over his words, he said, 'How can you save others if you haven't first saved yourself?'

He has a point.

MORAL

Learn to cherish yourself and others equally.

REFLECTION

You can use this story to illustrate issues such as influencing, assertiveness, self-esteem and personal achievement.

Do you cherish yourself as well as others?
In what ways do you demonstrate that you cherish yourself?
How do you feel about cherishing yourself – guilty?
How do you, or someone you know, relate to other people – assertive, aggressive or passive?
Assertiveness is about finding a balance between your own needs and those of others. Do you achieve this balance?

50

INTRODUCTION

This story, written by Louise Arthur, was quoted in Storylines, *the magazine of the Society for Storytelling in the United Kingdom. Louise Arthur was a young woman who was a very promising writer. She died sadly of cancer early in the spring of 2000. In this sometimes less than beautiful world, I was touched with the dignity of the writer and the beauty of the sentiments.*

THE TALE

A Final Note...

We've just been to a storytelling session at a local theatre. It was wonderful to be absorbed into the world of magic. I was not a woman with cancer; I was a warrior princess in a fairytale fighting magical beasts.

This body, with its eye patch and walking stick, that feels so ungainly, was light and fit again, capable of feats of strength and magical power. On the way home, the sun broke through the clouds and anything seemed possible.

MORAL

The power of storytelling goes on forever...

REFLECTION

This story can be used to discuss such issues as self-esteem, self-image, limiting and empowering beliefs, and inner calm.

In what way can you relate to the story?
What type of language do you use to describe yourself and others?
How does your self-esteem affect your description of yourself and others?
Is this language helpful and accurate?
How might you want to change your own self-image?

References and Further Reading

Baker, A and Greene, E (1977) *Storytelling: Art and technique*, RR Bowker and Company, New York

Bartter, M, Hilgartner, C and Stoneman, M (1999) *The Importance of Storytelling to Time-binding*, http://www.hilgart.org/papers

Bell, C R (1992) The trainer as storyteller, *Training and Development*, September, pp 53–56

Bennis, W (1996) The leader as storyteller, *Harvard Business Review*, **74** (1), pp 154–61

Bettelheim B (1991) *The Uses of Enchantment: The meaning and importance of fairy tales*, Penguin, London

Boje, D (1999) *Narrative Therapy*, http://web.mnsu.edu/~dboje

Boller, K and Rovee-Collier, C (1992) Contextual coding and recoding of infants' memories, *Journal of Experimental Child Psychology*, **53** (1), pp 1–23

Burch, M (1997) *Storytelling: It's not just kid's stuff!*, Kind Crone Productions, e-mail: Kindcrone@aol.com

Campbell, J (1993) *The Hero with a Thousand Faces*, Fontana Press, London

Canfield, J (1996) *Heart at Work*, McGraw-Hill, New York

Canfield, J, *Chicken Soup for the Soul* series, Health Communications Inc

Colwell, E (1980) *Storytelling*, Bodley Head, London

Cook, M (1999) *Effective Coaching*, McGraw-Hill, New York

Covey, S (1992) *The Seven Habits of Highly Effective People*, Simon & Schuster, London

Csikszentmihalyi, M (1990) *Flow: The psychology of optimal experience*, Harper & Row, New York

Deikman, A (1982) *The Observing Self*, Beacon Press, Boston

Dryden, G and Vos, J (1994) *The Learning Revolution*, Accelerated Learning Systems, Aylesbury

Finlay, M and Hogan, C (1995) 'Who will bell the cat?' Storytelling techniques for people who work with people in organisations, *Training and Management Development Methods*, **9**, pp 6.01–6.18

Goleman, D (1999) *Working with Emotional Intelligence*, Bloomsbury, London

Handy, C (1995) *Beyond Certainty*, Hutchinson, London

Hannaford, C (1995) *Smart Moves: Why learning is not all in your head*, Great Ocean Publishers, Atlanta

Hattersley, M (1997) The managerial art of telling a story, *Harvard Management Update*, January

Jensen, E (1988) *Superteaching*, Turning Point Press, San Diego, California

Jensen, E (1995) *The Learning Brain*, Turning Point Press, San Diego, California

Kaye, B and Jacobson, B (1999) True tales and tall tales, *Training and Development*, March, pp 45–50

Kolb, D A (1984) *Experiential Learning Experiences as the Source of Learning and Development*, Prentice-Hall, New York

Lakoff, G and Johnson, M (1980) *Metaphors We Live By*, University of Chicago Press, Chicago

McCann, D and Stewart, J (1997) *Aesop's Fables*, Butterworth-Heinemann, Oxford

McGaugh, J L *et al*, (1990) Involvement of the Amygdaloid complex in neuromodulatory influences on memory storage, *Neuroscience and Biobehavioural Reviews*, **14** (4), pp 425–31

Mellon, N (1992) *Storytelling and the Art of Imagination*, Element Books, Shaftesbury

Molden, D (1996) *Managing with the Power of NLP*, Pearson Education, London

Neuhauser, P (1993) *Corporate Legends and Lore*, McGraw-Hill, New York

O'Connor, J and Seymour, J (1990) *Introducing Neuro-Linguistic Programming*, HarperCollins, London

O'Keefe, J and Nadel, L (1978) *The Hippocampus as a Cognitive Map*, Oxford Clarendon Press, Oxford

Ornstein, R (1977) *The Psychology of Consciousness*, Penguin, New York

Parkin, M (1998) *Tales for Trainers*, Kogan Page, London

Parsloe, E and Wray, M (2000) *Coaching and Mentoring*, Kogan Page, London

Peter, L and Dana, B (1982) *The Laughter Prescription*, Ballantine Books, New York

Rodenburg, P (1992) *The Right to Speak*, Methuen Drama, London

Rodenburg, P (1993) *The Need for Words*, Methuen Drama, London

Rosen, B (1988) *And None of it was Nonsense*, Mary Glasgow Publications

Rosen, H (1982) *My Voice will Go with You*, WW Norton, New York

Rosen, H (1987), *Stories and Meanings*, David Green, Northampton

Simmerman, S (1997) *Teaching the Caterpillar to Fly*, Performance Management Company, Taylors, South Carolina, www.simmerman.com

Sperry, R (1968) Hemisphere disconnection and unity in conscious awareness, *American Psychologist*, **23**, pp 723–33

von Oech, R (1998) *A Whack on the Side of the Head*, Warner Books, New
York

Watts, N (1996) *Storyscape*, www.ccweb.co.uk.telling.html

Zipes, J (1996) *Revisiting the Storyteller*, Daylight Press, London

Useful Addresses and Contacts

STORYTELLING ORGANIZATIONS

For general information on storytelling, contact:

Australian Storytelling Guild (NSW) Inc.
PO Box 321
Drummoyne
New South Wales
Australia
e-mail: stories@s504aone.net.au

Folklore Society Library
University College London
Gower Street
London
WC1E 6BT

School of Scottish Studies
The University of Edinburgh
27 St George Square
Edinburgh
Scotland
EH8 9LD

Society for Storytelling
PO Box 2344
Reading
Berkshire
RG6 7FG

The National Storytelling Network
116 1/2 West Main Street
Jonesborough
Tennessee 37659
USA
e-mail: nsn@naxs.net

The Ulster-American Folk Park Library
Mellon Road
Castletown
Omagh
Co Tyrone
BT78 5QY

Welsh Folk Museum Library
Llyfrell Amgueddfa Werin Cymru
St Fagans
Cardiff
Wales
CF5 6XB

For training workshops on storytelling and articles on storytelling, contact:

Barry McWilliams and Chuck Larkin
http://www.seanet.com/~eldrbarry/roos/st_defn.htm
e-mail: eldrbarry@eldrbarry.seanet.com

Doug Lipman
http://www.storypower.com

Jim Woodward
http://storyteller.net

Margaret Parkin
Training Options
50 Landing Lane
Hemingbrough
Selby
North Yorkshire
YO8 6RA
e-mail: training_options@msn.com
Web site: http://www.trainingoptionsuk.com

Milbre Burch
Kind Crone Productions
e-mail: kindcrone@aol.com

Pat Williams
MindField Seminars
The Barn
Church Farm
Chalvington
East Sussex
BN27 3TD

Jo Radner
President of the American Folklore Society
http://www.afsnet.org

OTHER USEFUL CONTACTS

For information about NLP, contact:

The Association for NLP
PO Box 78
Stourbridge
West Midlands
DY8 2YP

For information about coaching, contact:

Coaching House
miranda@coachinghouse.com

International Coach Federation
icfoffice@coachfederation.org

Life Coaching Academy
info@lifecoachingacademy.com

Thomas J Leonard
Chief Executive Officer
http://www.thomasleonard.com

Index